THE
Courage
OF A
WOMAN

JUNE CURTIS

To Zip,

Clothe yourself daily
with His courage!

Gen. 27:14

I love you,
June Curtis

HARVEST HOUSE PUBLISHERS
Eugene, Oregon 97402

THE COURAGE OF A WOMAN

Copyright © 1990 by Harvest House Publishers
Eugene, Oregon 97402

Library of Congress Cataloging-in-Publication Data

Curtis, June.
ISBN 0-89081-786-3
   1. Women—Religious life.   2. Courage—Religious aspects—Christianity.
  1. Title.
   BV4527.C85   1990
  248.8′43—dc20   89-38599
                                                  CIP

Printed in the United States of America.

*This book is dedicated
to my beloved grandchildren:*

*Joseph, Jessica, Derek, Dustin,
Devin and Matthew, and Micah.
I pray you will become men and women
filled with God-given courage.*

Contents

Do not ask to have your life's
   load lightened,
But for courage to endure.
Do not ask for fulfillment in all
   your life,
But for patience to accept frustrations.
Do not ask for perfection in all you do,
But for the wisdom not to repeat mistakes.
And finally, do not ask for more,
Before saying "Thank You" for what
   you have already received.

—Brenda Short

Preface

"Hurry up and finish. I need it!" That is the response I heard time and again as I told people about this book. Strangers would approach me after a retreat or conference, pleading with me to write a book on God-given courage and how to obtain it. A friend whose husband had lost his company, another whose husband was unemployed, a third whose husband had suddenly filed for divorce and a fourth who was in the midst of raising several children all begged me to complete this project as of yesterday.

The problems of both strangers and acquaintances have ranged from facing a geographical change in their living situation to whether to go back to school or work to staying in a difficult marriage or whether even to get married. At times, the situations presented were readily answerable and the principles for courage easy to apply. Then there were the heartaches and heartbreaks that made me feel as though "all the king's horses and all the king's men could not put them back together again."

Yet one by one, as we worked through Bible-based guidelines regarding God-given courage, we discovered these time-tested principles still work. They worked for Joseph, Moses, Ruth, Jochabed, Mary the mother of Jesus, Jeremiah, David, Naaman, Paul and even Jesus, and they are still valid today.

It is my conviction that too often these principles are forgotten or misapplied so we throw them overboard, believing them to be impotent or outdated. But God did not present us with ineffective guidelines, nor does He keep changing the rules on us. Have you ever played a game with someone who kept misapplying or misinterpreting the rules to his/her advantage? Well, rest assured, our Lord does *not* operate that way.

If you are feeling defeated and are ready to give up, please, please read on and apply God's biblical ingredients for saturating yourself with Divine courage. You have nothing to lose and *everything* to gain.

Acknowledgments

A book of any size requires the understanding and patience of everyone whose life the author touches. Since the inception of this book, everyone has been encouraging and helpful, even when I felt like filing it permanently in the discard file.

My eternal thanks:

To faithful friends who graciously allowed me to share their stories with you

To Becky, my editor at *Virtue* magazine, for her steady stream of understanding

To Eileen and Bob at Harvest House who believed in this project

To Pastor John and Patti for their well-timed concern

To Beth who is truly a prime example of Godly courage

To Carol who helped the book get "off the ground"

To family members who allowed me to hibernate when necessary

To my husband Rich for his assistance and constant "pats on the back" as my cheerleader

And last but certainly not least,

To Jesus Christ for showing me His promise contained in John 7:37 during one period of discouragement... "Rivers of living water shall flow from the inmost being of anyone who believes in Me." Thanks, Lord, I needed that!

***Always remember
to ask for and receive
God-given courage.***

*God is our refuge and strength, a tested help in
times of trouble. And so we need not fear even if
the world blows up, and the mountains crumble
into the sea.*

—Psalm 46:1,2

1

The Necessary Ingredient

Fearlessness. Tenacity. Valor. Grit. Solid, powerful words to describe the ingredient vital to the fulfilling of life—courage. Without it, we become empty, quivering forms of humanity tossed about by the storms of adversity that inevitably come our way.

An endless onslaught of headlines bombards us with the threats of nuclear holocaust, AIDS, crime and drugs, giving us daily cause for faintness of heart. The equilibrium of our faith is further upset when we are personally touched by a tragic or perhaps not-so-tragic, but unplanned, occurrence. Let me ask you the following question:

Are you afraid of courage?

Whenever I read or hear of people reacting courageously in harrowing situations, I wonder what principles they used to put courage into action. I also am curious as to whether they're even aware that their courage is God's gift to them.

Several years ago, newspapers carried the remarkable story of one young woman's brave triumph in adversity. A sailing trip to Hawaii with a friend turned to tragedy when they found themselves at the mercy of a fierce storm in the Pacific Ocean. While they sought shelter in the boat's small cabin, a huge wave struck and capsized the craft.

The friend was never seen again. After battling her way out of the cabin through debris and a flooded compartment door, the young woman climbed on top of what remained of the sailboat. For days, which stretched into weeks, she held on tenaciously with little food and only rain water to drink. Finally after drifting for almost a month, she was spotted off the coast of Hawaii and was rescued.

In the ensuing interviews she repeatedly said, "I knew I would make it," or "I was determined to make it." I greatly admired her courage as I read her story, and I longed to find out more about how she found the strength to survive.

I wish I could always be that brave and stouthearted. Too often my knees feel like jelly and my backbone seems to dissolve. At times, my courage fails during even the most minor occurrences, such as confronting a barking dog on an evening walk. Occasionally, with fear and trembling, I'll continue on past the villainous hound. Usually, however, I retreat and walk another route. And I know I'm not alone in these feelings. I have observed other people walking, carrying clubs or small cans of mace to fight back with in case of attack by man or beast.

Daily Courage

We are challenged to use courage, to some degree, daily... in our marriages, in our roles as parents, in our responses to moral issues, even first thing in the morning. For most of us it takes a certain amount of courage to look at ourselves in the mirror after wrestling with the blankets and pillows all night!

It takes courage to discipline ourselves to eat the right food for breakfast. If we have children in the home, it often takes a huge dose of courage to face the day with them. "What's for breakfast, Mom?" "What did you pack for my lunch today?" "Oh, I've told you a hundred times, I hate leftovers!" "Where is my homework?" "Where's my other shoe?" On and on until we want to flee to a more tranquil place. Courageously we hang in there, placing their needs above ours.

Shakespeare wrote that "courage mounteth with occasion." It takes different amounts of courage to deal with diverse arenas of life, ranging from decisions about what movies to see to lifelong choices of whether to remain single or get married. For example, if the choice or circumstances point to remaining unmarried, courage is required to keep one's self pure and to lead a celibate life; if the choice is marriage, courage is needed to keep that commitment even through the cloudy and stormy days.

Maintaining purity in marriage takes a constant stream of courage as our society becomes more and more sexually permissive. What appear to be exciting sexual experiences outside the marriage bed are portrayed over and over on television, in magazines, in novels and by the lifestyles of well-known celebrities. Christians inadvertently become influenced by the world and its mores. To stay true to godly values for marriage, we need courage to act on the Spirit's prompting and strive for the Lord's righteousness.

When it comes to preserving our moral integrity, whether married or single, God-given courage beyond our own is vital. When we become passive and self-assured in this area, we're "inviting trouble," as the saying goes. It takes courage to deny ungodly images access to our minds through what we see. It takes courage to close our ears to music that is jarring to our spiritual natures. It takes courage to deny ourselves Christ-forbidden emotional experiences, to combat the world's mentality that "if it feels good, do it." To be a Christian and to be divided in this area brings about instability in every facet of our lives. James 1:8 says,

"A double minded man (or woman) *is* unstable in all his (or her) ways" (KJV).

Giving Birth to Courage

A natural progression for most couples after marriage is to have children. Whether planned or not, courage is required in this experience as well. Since abortion is a readily available alternative in today's world, to have a child while engulfed in difficulties is courageous. Single women who become pregnant, married women in less-than-ideal circumstances, Christian or not, face the same choice—whether to allow the fetus to develop into a productive life.

Even as a happily married woman, giving birth to our children required a large portion of God-given courage for me. After becoming pregnant, my initial reaction was the same all four times. Oh, no, nine months of watching my body deteriorate as it expands. Nine months of feeling "yucky" off and on, growing increasingly uncomfortable and knowing I would be waddling like a duck before the process was complete.

As I listened to other women share "war stories" of their deliveries, especially during my first pregnancy, fear took over to the point of producing nightmares. Anxiety about real as well as imagined concerns dominated my mind, and controlled my body.

One particular night is still vividly etched in my memory, more than 30 years later. The sounds of my own sobbing woke me as I cried out, "No, no, no!" My husband tenderly embraced me and held my trembling body close to his.

"Honey, what's the matter? Everything's okay, Junie." I tearfully confided that I had dreamed our baby would be born without arms. The dream was very realistic, but Rich kept reassuring me that it was *only* a dream and that our baby would be perfect. I wanted desperately to believe him.

If I could fully trust in Rich's words, why couldn't I then trust Almighty God into whose life I had been reborn through Jesus Christ?

When the time for the birth of our first child arrived, Rich, for all his reassurances, was working across town. My cousin Mary assisted me to the hospital and I remember saying to her in a panicked voice, "Is there any way I can get out of this? I don't want to go through it!" Laughingly she replied, "Well, you should have thought of that nine months ago." Some comfort, huh?

I did go into a state of shock and cried, shook, got sick, became angry at Rich, and overwhelmingly felt sorry for myself. As the doctor and nurses took charge, I discovered I had no other choice but to cooperate and work with them. Instinctively I knew that the more I listened to their advice, the sooner the dreaded endeavor would become our blessed event.

No, it wasn't a fun, painless experience but the end product was and is one of the greatest joys of my life—my daughter Krystal. Twenty-four years later, I had the special privilege of assisting her when she delivered our first grandchild, a curly-haired angel named Joseph.

The cycle of giving birth in the physical realm is parallel to allowing the Lord, through the progression of our walk with Him, to birth spiritual growth and development in our lives. When we invite Him into our hearts, He implants His seed in us. As we allow Him the freedom to bring about spiritual maturity, we must be willing to let Christ use the good, the bad and the ugly situations we go through.

Often we cry, "No, I can't go through this. Is there a way out immediately?" When my ability to continue in labor was at its lowest point, God-given courage took over although I did not recognize it as such at the time. I had no choice but to release my own desires.

I was not aware to what extent we would need His faithfulness in the realm of courage until about a week after the delivery. Mistakenly, I thought after that period of time, the

trying times would end and we could get back to "normal."
How wrong I was. Things have never again been "normal"
for Rich and me!

The Necessity for Continual Courage

The bulk of courage you will need will involve ordinary,
day to day circumstances of life. There will also be times,
however, for they come to all of us, when you face difficulties so severe that you may question your faith in God,
His love and your purpose for even existing.

During these painful periods the courage required often
retreats to a dark, unknown corner of one's life or is purposely ignored. Self-pity, fear, anger, diminished self-worth,
insecurities or acts of rebellion commonly dominate, cloud-
ing a person's walk with the Lord and stealing his or her joy
away.

Reactions to life's challenging circumstances vary widely,
but we'll place them in two general categories: negative or
positive. To always respond in a positive, courageous manner *out of our own strength* is nearly impossible. If the
principles that we will discuss throughout the book are not
followed the majority of the time, a negative, man-made
solution will appear to be the only way out.

It is interesting as well as reassuring to read biblical
accounts of individuals' and entire nations' honest reactions to difficult circumstances. It will be my overall
purpose to emphasize the men and women who responded
positively in fear-causing situations, but I readily admit
that there are exceptions, even in God's Word.

The Israelites looked time and again for man-made solutions. Temptation, pride, stubbornness, disobedience, fear
and self-indulgence were often their choices in hard times.
Yet God's patience, mercy and grace toward them is displayed over and over in the Old Testament. In Jeremiah
32:27 He asks them, "Is there anything too hard for me?" He
continues to remind the people of their failures and sins,

but concludes the chapter with a promise of restoration, blessing and faithfulness.

What a wonderful Lord! He tells us too, "For I know the plans I have for you, says the Lord. They are plans for good and not for evil, to give you a future and a hope" (Jeremiah 29:11). But like the children of Israel, we tend to be short-sighted when it comes to looking beyond the present and remaining patient for the Lord to act. Too often our present and future seem so pressure-filled and uncertain that we are overcome, not by God-given courage, but by depression, disobedience and trumped-up man-made solutions.

Allowing God in Your Boat

The sixth chapter of Mark presents an exciting example of the Lord's courage overriding that of some of His disciples, leaving them aghast and amazed. While He prayed in the hills above the Sea of Galilee, a storm suddenly blew the calm waters into rough waves, threatening to upset the boat His disciples were rowing below. He saw they were in serious trouble, struggling against the elements.

As He walked on the water past their boat, they became more frightened of Him than of the storm. The Bible says that when they saw what seemed to be a ghost, they screamed. Fright of the storm suddenly became secondary as they faced the specter of something in the dark they could not explain. How like human nature to be engulfed by fear, but how like Christ to say, "It's all right. It is I. Don't be afraid."

Then He did something else. He climbed into the boat with them. The moment He got on board the wind ceased and the waters became smooth. Those very human disciples had some very human reactions. First, they couldn't fully comprehend what they had just gone through. The situation that had been topsy-turvy and life-threatening moments before was now suddenly quiet and tranquil. What a contrast!

Second, they did not recognize that the figure who climbed into the boat with them was Jesus. They had not fully understood that when He became a part of their lives they became heir to His protection, presence, peace and courage.

The first and most important principle toward appropriating divine courage is to allow God to climb into the boat with you. For Him to do that, you must belong to His family. This is accomplished by recognizing your inability to live the way you should on your own strength. The disciples could not row their boat against the storm and neither can you. Know that when you give Jesus Christ permission to enter your life, you inherit the same attributes the disciples did—His protection, presence, calm and courage.

Long ago a Naval captain and his crew were sailing the waters off an enemy shore in South America. As they drew closer to land, heavy artillery came into view. Fear gripped the men and they abandoned their ship's guns and ran for the lifeboats on the opposite side. The captain shouted orders and waved them back to their posts, but to no avail.

Finally out of desperation he turned to his wife and asked if she would take her place beside one of the ship's cannons and fire it if necessary. Without hesitation she sprinted to the nearest gun and waited for further orders. The men who were abandoning ship noticed this frail little woman facing the same enemy that had frightened them to the point of desertion.

Embarrassed but possessing newly-found courage due to her example, they took up their posts again and defeated the enemy. Later, one of the men asked this brave woman how she was able to follow the orders they had run from. She replied, "I looked at the calm on my husband's face."

Who among us hasn't tried mustering up courage out of our human reservoir? Which of us has never resorted to our own devices? Whenever I've chosen those two routes, I have found there is never enough courage and it always fails me at the most inopportune times. I want to run for the lifeboats instead of standing my ground against the Enemy.

But more than ever, I am convinced that there is *no* circumstance in life for which we have to accept defeat and there isn't anything that can keep us from receiving God-given courage if we choose to acquire it. In today's world, it is vital for us to keep looking into the calm face of our Almighty Captain and obey His orders. For it is only in Him that we gain supernatural strength and determination to face tomorrow.

Measuring Your "Courage Quotient"

As you journey through this book, read it as though you are looking into a unique kind of mirror. For instead of examining the outward appearance, the questions asked in each chapter will measure your internal "courage quotient."

Steps to Becoming a Courageous Woman

1. Invite the Lord to become the most important ingredient in your life if you have not done so.

2. List the areas of your life that are producing fear and possibly causing panic.

3. Read Mark 6:46-52 and draw parallels to your life.

4. Pray, asking the Lord to climb into the boat with you and calm the storms in your life.

5. Memorize Psalm 46:1,2. Meditate on how the verses apply to your situation.

Do not be afraid to ask for and receive God-given courage.

***Stand firm in Christ
in the midst of negative
circumstances.***

*Yes, though a mighty army marches against me,
my heart shall know no fear! I am confident that
God will save me.*

—Psalm 27:3

2

Hanging By a Thread

God-given courage involves a choice—one that is often born out of persistence conceived in desperation. The freedom to choose is one of the fantastic privileges we receive when we are released from the clutches of self-sufficiency into the protective arms of a loving Heavenly Father.

The act of choosing divine courage is an on-going process, not a once and for all decision. How much easier it would be if all our difficulties could be solved in one instant, such as "the magic wand" theory I heard recently. The idea was put forth that God could "wave His holy magic wand" and make all our problems disappear if He wanted to.

Yes, I suppose He could work "magically" in our situations. Instead, because of His great love for us, He desires to bring about growth, maturity and long-term benefits in our lives. He knows that as long as we're a part of planet earth, we will feel pressure on our spiritual tires as we travel life's road. He is always at the ready to inflate them and even retread our faith when needed.

Persistence to choose courage is often overcome by discouragement. With regard to whatever difficulty you are facing today, how would you answer the following question?

Have you given up?

To give up is to surrender to the forces that are overpowering us, whether they involve people or circumstances. There are times when it is best to give up, such as yielding our rights and wills to the Lord's control. To give ourselves totally into His management is one of the main ingredients for living a fulfilling Christian life.

The question I am asking, however, addresses a sense of defeatism, a succumbing to the difficulties facing you. Perhaps you feel the Enemy has rolled over you with his artillery, his tanks and all the ammunition and weapons of warfare at his disposal. He has you right where he wants you, backed into a corner where you may be cowering. He gleefully applauds his ability to destroy, defeat and on occasion, devastate his opponent.

Did you notice, however, the confidence exuded by the author of Psalm 27:3, in the opening verse of this chapter? Even though he knew what it was to be surrounded by the enemy, he was no longer afraid. He knew Whose he was and where his salvation would come from. He knew that what he lacked in fighting skills would be compensated by his Heavenly Commander.

Maximizing Our Deficiencies

I recently read of a high school wrestler who was born with only one arm. Whenever he faced opponents who were unfamiliar with him, they made unkind remarks concerning his disability and the ease with which they planned to defeat him. To their surprise, he pinned nearly every one of them. You see, he strengthened the parts of his body that he did have instead of being incapacitated by the one arm he didn't have. In fact, he claimed that his missing arm made it more difficult for his opponents to hold him and make the wrestling moves that would defeat him. He used the rules of the sport and his disability to his advantage.

Before joining the team and putting in the long hours of practice, this young man was failing his academic courses. Yet as he discovered he could be a winner in one area of his life, he became a winner in another. His grades improved dramatically. He bravely tried a difficult sport, one that requires skill and strength. He had the courage not only to win over his opponents, but also over his defeatist attitude.

What an example of choosing courage! When we fail to make a conscious decision to work at choosing courage, we can become immobilized with fear or an "I don't care" attitude. We give up and throw our lives into neutral, lapsing into a type of spiritual, emotional and/or mental limbo. The danger of becoming "numb" in our circumstances is that it makes us insensitive to the Holy Spirit. We become vulnerable to every potentially negative plot Satan throws at us. Our ability to make wise decisions is weakened, and we suffer even deeper discouragement. Our bad situations often become more pronounced or prolonged. We feel as though we're dangling at the end of a rope.

Climbing Rocks and Obtaining Courage

This principle was vividly portrayed to me a few months ago when Rich and I visited a spectacularly beautiful place in Oregon known as Smith Rock State Park. Rock climbers, from novice to expert, travel there from various parts of the world to try their climbing skills. As I studied the dozens of individuals scaling the high walls that appeared to have been sliced by a giant machete, I was struck by the parallels for acquiring God-given courage.

Human courage manifested itself in that park through a combination of being and doing. The climbers had to *be* extremely cautious and they had to *do* the correct climbing procedures. In the physical realm, man's courage seemed sufficient.

It took more courage than I could imagine to climb several hundred feet straight up a rock wall, but immediately I noticed the climbers were well-prepared for the challenge. They had specially designed equipment—proper shoes, clothing, rope, pitons and carabiners (clamps that fasten to the rope).

Only the foolish would have started to climb without first receiving thorough instruction. Then each one had to follow the instructions as if their lives depended on it—and they did! The climbers all began in safety at the bottom of the rocks and as they gained confidence and experience, they climbed higher and higher. Most of them followed in the tracks of those who had gone before. A few more-experienced or perhaps more daring climbers pursued unmarked routes that looked increasingly difficult.

I observed that their ropes were the climbers' most important piece of equipment. They were literally their life-lines. The climbers were always connected to their lines, which were then held by a "buddy." The "buddy" system seemed very necessary in securing a safe hold for each one. We saw a few people slip and fall, but they all escaped serious injury because they were secured by a partner and a good strong rope.

Those climbers vividly illustrated human courage, the type depicting the innate survival instinct placed by God in each of us. But every person I saw demonstrating courage that day seemed to be in control of his or her situation. What of the "climbs" in our life during which we lose control and slip or fall? What type of courage is most effective then?

I have decided that rock climbing is not for the faint-of-heart and neither is life. God has provided us with the right equipment through His Son Jesus Christ and His Holy Spirit who lives in us when we give Him permission. He has given us His Word as our Book of Instructions to face the challenges of life. We too must follow the guidelines as though our lives depend on it—for they do!

Experience is gained when we walk step by step with our Savior and gain confidence that He will never allow more than we can face, with His help, to enter our days. A deeper trust level will only come about when we're challenged by rocky or rough situations. We can also learn from fellow "climbers" who have learned God's principles and the importance of their application.

Our climbing rope or "lifeline" is our relationship to the Lord. He desires that we constantly recognize Him as our Source of rescue. There are times, however, when holding on to that line seems impossible.

That's where prayer comes in. It is the resin, the "gripper" that enables us to hang on to our rope when we feel ourselves falling or giving up. Even if we're dangling in "space," prayer will help us hold onto our faith and its Author. The right "buddy," one who will uphold you in prayer, is also vitally important. If you lack someone to fill this role for you, ask the Lord to send the right person into your life. Let it be His choice. This person should be godly, yet not play God in your life. He or she should be sensitive to your needs, but remain more aware of God's Word and work. Your "buddy" should be loving, yet not condescending.

Persistence Pays

A woman whose dogged determination for healing as recorded in Luke 8 and Mark 5 provides an amazing example of tenacity. She had been plagued by a bleeding problem for 12 years and after trying all the remedies suggested by the doctors of her day, she finally sought help from Jesus.

She was undoubtedly in a constant state of fatigue and was more than likely shunned by her husband, if she had one, for being "unclean." Perhaps her condition interfered with her ability to bear children. At any rate, she was in a miserable state, but it was her disability that brought her to Jesus.

The crowds pressed tightly around Him that day. I can imagine her pushing her way through until standing on tiptoes, with her frail arms extended, she was finally able to make physical contact. Perhaps she felt a new warmth surge through her body as instantly she knew she was rid of her scourge. Just the touching of Jesus brought miraculous healing to her life. But she had to catch the lifeline He threw to her.

I'm aware that the accounts in both Mark and Luke sound as though Jesus did not know who touched Him. Of course, He did! He is an omniscient God. I believe He wanted her to admit to herself and everyone standing nearby that day where her healing had originated. For her sake, He made a point of her confession. In doing so, He let her know that her "not-giving-up" faith was rewarded.

Having Courage When Healing Does Not Occur

My youngest sister, Marvel, is an inspiration to her family and friends because she has also reached out to the God of miracles. Yet instead of healing her from the trauma of nerve damage that occurred at birth, He has graced her with courage time and again to face a world where others have often been cruel and unaccepting.

While bravely living alone in an apartment, she must combat loneliness, misunderstanding neighbors, a very limited income, hard-to-read recipes and limited job skills. As a result, she has adapted to a lifestyle of potential boredom in simple, yet creative ways.

She rides the bus all around the rather large city in which she resides, in addition to bicycling and walking. The church she enjoys attending is a walk of several miles each way, but she doesn't complain even if the weather is bad.

Her keen sense of humor is often the source of hearty laughter by those around her. Her life—a picture of patience, trust, unconditional love and faith in her Creator—humbles me constantly. She never complains about her disadvantages or indulges in pity parties. Although she too has reached out and touched Jesus, just as the woman with the bleeding problem, He has had another plan for her life. She is content knowing that He is always with her. Rather than giving up or retreating, she faces life every moment of the day as its challenges come her way.

If you are in a situation that appears to have no solution and you feel you are trapped on a sheer precipice with no way up or down, reach out and touch Jesus. As you grab onto the lifeline He is extending to you today, through persistently applying His principles, you too will become a woman of courage. The choice is yours.

Steps to Becoming a Courageous Woman

1. Read the story in Luke 8:43-48 and Mark 5:25-34 of the determined woman mentioned in this chapter.

2. Write down the ways that let you know she had not "given up."

3. If you have "given up" or are gripped by inaction, pray, asking the Lord to restore your hope in Him.

4. Begin today to apply the principles taught in this chapter.

5. Memorize Psalm 27:3.

Stand firm in Christ in the
midst of negative circumstances.

❦

Refuse to let fear dominate your life.

Even when we are too weak to have any faith left, he remains faithful to us and will help us, for he cannot disown us who are part of himself, and he will always carry out his promises to us.

—2 Timothy 2:13

3

Momentary Decisions Produce Everlasting Results

In his book, *In Search of the Cross*, Robert J. Weiland writes:

> Jesus had a will of His own that was naturally opposed to bearing the cross, just as I have a will of my own that is likewise opposed. He said openly, "Not as I will." What He did is as clear as sunlight: He denied His own will. Further, it is plain that it was impossible for Him to follow His Father's will until He first denied His own will, because the two were in direct conflict. They formed a cross.[1]

Each of us will inevitably face a crossroads that will form our cross. Our response will reveal whose will is controlling us—ours or His.

Until that is resolved, effective Christian living is not accomplished. God knows that step is vital. If it was necessary for His Son, is it any less important for us, His redeemed children? Faithfulness and love compel Him to provide courage through the decision-making process, but often it is obscured by our fears.

Does fear dominate your life?

When we taught our children to ride their bicycles, they started out with training wheels on the back and one of us running alongside to catch them in case of a spill. We did not hand them the challenge and then stand back and laugh, watching their vain attempts at keeping their balance. Would God do any less?

One of the major causes of depression is that when we are confronted by a decision that will affect our behavior, even if it is relatively minor, we panic because we feel our "bike is tipping over" and there is no one to catch us. The resulting anxiety and apprehension can make us physically ill and emotionally crippled to varying degrees. Distrust of our own or another's abilities causes fear and a "down" feeling. Depression *really* sets in when we distrust our Heavenly Father.

This can happen especially in relation to our concern for our families. Also, if you are employed outside the home you probably encounter situations that require daily courage in the workplace. Fear of an employer, other employees or feelings of your own inadequacies can make you so nervous and tension-ridden that you cannot work to your maximum potential.

Fear to Use Talents

Often we're depressed because we realize the gifts or talents God has freely given us are being hidden due to fear of failure. Individuals with thrilling testimonies of what the Lord has done in their lives remain silent because of fear.

Some people are afraid to give themselves or material possessions to the Lord for fear their motives will be misinterpreted.

I'm certain most of us are acquainted with "closet" musicians who are afraid to share their talents for fear of ridicule. Secret, gifted writers abound but are fearful of rejection so no one is allowed to gain from their reservoirs of knowledge. In all of these cases, not only the individuals but the whole Body of Christ loses out because of fear.

Fear Caused by Debt

America is a nation of huge, perhaps insurmountable indebtedness because millions of us have lacked the courage to deny ourselves something until we could afford it. This has been true on a national level, but more directly we as members of the Body of Christ charge, borrow and even deny Christ His fair share so we can pay for another luxury. Societal pressure, whether real or self-imposed, becomes greater than our wisdom and the common sense that Solomon wrote about in Proverbs 3:21, "Have two goals; wisdom—that is, knowing and doing right—and common sense." He goes on to admonish us: "Don't let them slip away." Fear has on many occasions caused us to let them slip away. Depression abounds over financial indebtedness.

Fear of the Ordinary

Driving or riding in a car requires courage, either consciously or subconsciously. One day as I was returning home from a speaking engagement in central Oregon fear became a very real foe. The trip included a mountain pass, in which the road twisted and wound past lakes and a river or two. Even though the drive was beautiful and picturesque, it demanded constant concentration, especially on corners where I frequently met trucks loaded with logs or cars whose drivers were pushing the accelerator too hard, hurtling their cars over the center line. Our 5-year-old daughter Karol was my companion on that particular journey.

Suddenly I was overcome with a feeling of dread that we were going to be killed in a terrible accident. Fear of what was ahead for us became so distracting that I began to shake. I found it difficult to even steer the car to the shoulder of the road to park. Between my tears and Karol's "Why are we stopping, Mommy?" I felt total panic. I, a person who prided herself in being "in control," not given to excessive worrying, was totally enveloped by fear.

As we walked down the embankment to a nearby lake, I with rubbery knees and Karol oblivious to impending doom, I began to envision us being held in God's huge hand. By His Spirit, He whispered to me that I need not fear because we were in His hands and that was all that I needed to remember. The feeling of calm and trust He offered took time for me to appropriate, but once I did we got back in the car and drove home uneventfully.

Fear Which Lowers Our Resolve to Say "No"

Fear can also cause us to make decisions that will have a far-reaching effect on others. The fear of not winning a gold medal in the 1988 Olympics in Korea apparently drove Ben Johnson to compromise and break the international code of ethics by taking illegal substances into his body. The shockwaves are still being felt by his fellow-athletes as well as the rest of the world. When our 4-year-old grandson Derek saw Ben Johnson's picture in *Sports Illustrated* he pointed and said, "Look, Mommy, there's that man who took drugs."

How much better if he could have said, "Look, Mommy, there's one of the fastest runners in the world." The steroid, stanozolol, has become Ben Johnson's notoriety. The saddest aspect of all is that he might have won without succumbing to the drug and the destructive power of fear.

The courage of a ship's captain to say "no" to alcohol would have spared the world the disaster of a huge oil spill in a magnificent Alaskan bay. Experts say it will be years before the shores return to normal, not to mention the fishing, the wildlife and the economy. This is another sad illustration of the devastation caused by one man's lack of courage, as the effects of his failure to exercise self-discipline will likely be felt by all of us sooner or later.

Far-reaching Effects

When our children were growing up, Rich and I tried to impress on them that every choice they made would touch someone else. The "new morality" statement, "It's your decision because it only affects you," is untrue. *Every* choice we make affects others, either negatively or positively.

The apostle Paul took his decision-making role seriously when he wrote to his fellow-Believers in Corinth, "We try to live in such a way that no one will ever be offended or kept back from finding the Lord by the way we act, so that no one can find fault with us and blame it on the Lord" (2 Corinthians 6:3).

When our son Kendall was 19, he was hired as a car salesman. One day a "customer" invited him to his home, which happened to be an enormous, elegant house located in the hills south of our city. Eager to befriend this potential buyer, Kendall took him up on his offer.

During their visit, Kendall noticed several strikingly attractive, well-dressed women who apparently also lived there. The man disappeared for a short time into one of the bedrooms and returned with a suitcase. He placed the suitcase on a table and called Kendall over to view its contents. To his astonishment, it was filled with thousands of dollars.

His new "friend" said, "Kendall, if you will make just one flight to San Diego and back for me, this money can be yours. You can also choose which of these women you want and she will take care of your every need."

A few days later, our son told me, "Mom, I had never seen so much money or such beautiful women! It sounded so easy and I must admit I was tempted.

"Just a quick trip to San Diego and back. Sounded so easy. But I knew for that kind of money it had to be drug-related. I remembered how you and Dad used to tell us that momentary decisions could last for a lifetime and hurt not only us but a whole lot of other people. That gave me the 'guts' to say no. It was hard because you know how broke I am, but I felt total relief when I said no."

We were riding in the car and I was driving when he related this incident, and I must tell you I almost drove off the road with excitement and joy. Some of what we had tried to teach the kids about godly principles had borne fruit! It provided the impetus for a courageous decision.

One of Jesus' disciples succumbed to an offer he couldn't refuse and for monetary gain and man's approval he betrayed the godly principles he had learned from God's Son. Instead of having the courage to say "no," he chose to betray the best Friend he ever had. The effects of his choice have rippled down through the centuries as the death of that Friend became the means to salvation for millions.

We are told that even though he later deeply regretted what he had done, it was too late. His choice had already set the events in motion. His remorse eventually drove him to suicide. What a sad, infamous ending to a potentially glorious life. His name has become synonymous with one who turns on a friend, a betrayer—a Judas.

When fear dominates, our lack of courage betrays us. It causes us to make wrong decisions that may affect us and

those whose lives we touch for a long time to come—
perhaps for eternity.

Steps to Becoming a Courageous Woman

1. List the decisions you need to make today.

2. Pray, asking the Lord for the proper motive for your decisions. Don't let them be based on fear.

3. Read Hebrews 11, often called the Faith Chapter, and examine the behavior of the individuals mentioned.

4. Write down the everlasting results of their decisions.

5. Memorize 2 Timothy 2:13. Claim its promises.

Refuse to let fear
dominate your life.

**Take responsibility
for negative circumstances
that are the result of poor
judgment on your part.**

*Those who trust in the Lord are steady as Mount
Zion, unmoved by any circumstance.*
                                        —Psalm 125:1

4

Taming Our Natures to Trust

Delores had her worst fears verified. Don was having an affair. Her bed became her haven from the cruel joke life had played on her and the locked bedroom door a citadel against the one who offended—her husband.

No amount of sweet persuasion, apologies, threats, enticements or logical explanations could draw her from her chosen cemetery. She wanted nothing more than to die. Her family, her responsibilities as wife and mother, her friends, her home and her love for the Lord faded from reality. Self-pity was appropriately named—a pit. All she could think of was how good a wife she had tried to be, not to mention a good Christian. How could God and Don do this wicked thing to her? Never again could she trust either.

She was determined to find a way to make them both sorry and she found it. After self-pity and the tears ran out, anger set in. Oh, she had heard many sermons on bitterness and what it can do when forgiveness is lacking, but they did not seem to apply in her case. The hurt was too great. Besides, the sermons were delivered by men who had never been injured so deeply.

She tried to pray through her sobs but only heard her words echo inside her aching, empty chest. "Where are you, God? Why?" Because her frustration had indeed turned to anger, she filed for divorce as soon as she was able. As the "innocent" party, the blame was totally on Don's shoulders and she made certain everyone knew it.

She turned their three teenagers against their father also. Her every waking thought was to make him pay for what he did, and she did so in many ways. Forgiveness, mercy, grace—all attributes possible through her Heavenly Father—were forgotten or ignored.

Although Delores' children did turn against their father, they did not "rise up and call her blessed" (Proverbs 31:28). On the contrary, as soon as they were able they left home for more pleasant surroundings, even though Don had given her their beautiful house. They dropped out of church and became disillusioned with Christianity. They rejected the God-ordained institution of marriage and began justifying their godless lifestyles.

Don repented and tried repeatedly to gain back the respect of his family, but Delores' bitterness and hurt ran too deep. Eventually he accepted the divorce and moved to another city to begin life anew, leaving Delores to live a life far inferior to what God desired for her.

Although their names have been changed, this is not an uncommon story. It has been repeated time and again. Even though Don's offense was the obvious one, Delores' response reaped unmeasured agony for herself as well as others. She lacked the courage to trust God *in* all things and heaped offense on top of offense. She negated the Lord's ability to repair the damage caused by the original wrong.

Trust Is the Key

Trust is only a five-letter word, but what a profound

difference it can make. Reread the opening verse to this chapter. It contains a dynamic parallel between trust in God and the stability of one's life.

The Psalmist declares that if we trust, we'll become as steady as a rock, as steady as Mt. Zion. Even though Mt. Zion has changed outwardly with the construction of the Mosque of Omar on the Temple site and other ensuing excavations, it has remained in the same geographical location for thousands of years. No matter how many wars have been fought around it or how often the elements have battered it, it has not moved.

Likewise, if we completely trust in God we can remain unmoved by circumstances. Oh, we might be changed somewhat, just as erosion and time have taken their toll on Mt. Zion, but inside we will remain solid in our faith.

Let's focus on the word "trust" some more. The *Merriam-Webster Dictionary* defines it as the assured reliance on the character, strength or truth of someone or something. It is confident hope. It is entrusting something to someone who has our best interest in mind. What a simple definition for such a life-changing action.

When we don't place absolute trust in our Savior we say to Him, "Well, I guess You want what's best for me and mine, but I'll reserve some room to maneuver in my circumstances. I've been told You'll always be there for me so, well, if I mess things up, then You can have a chance at it!"

We may not say those actual words, but isn't that how we often react when we find ourselves in a predicament? Then you know the next step—to place all the blame on Him. We have to blame someone, don't we?

The events in our lives may be quite ordinary—a flat tire, burned cake, torn shirt, traffic ticket or bank overdraft. Whatever the circumstances, a negative response only compounds the problem. It never helps or solves anything, and usually clouds our judgment. We need to ask ourselves, *"Are negative circumstances a result of poor judgment on our part?"*

Lack of courage to fully trust the Lord usually results in impulsive, rash and emotional behavior. Admittedly, to always respond correctly is difficult, especially if we are the independent, impulsive type or if we are relying solely on the human dimension of courage. However, as we mature in Christ and become better acquainted with His nature, trusting should come more naturally. Sometimes, though, just when we think we fully trust, (boom! crash! ouch!) we take a tumble!

The Devil *Made* Me Do It!

We deceive ourselves when we blame someone else for our bad choices or poor reactions. Our Enemy, Satan, delights in deflecting the blame on our behalf just as he did in Eve's situation. In Genesis, chapter 3, we read how she responded to her circumstances with extremely poor judgment and then refused to accept the blame.

Eve and her husband Adam lived in the most beautiful earthly location ever created by God because it was perfect. Imagine, no problems—yet! One day, however, Satan disguised himself as a snake and said, "You know, Eve, you have a definite problem here. This is your place and you have all this delicious fruit at your fingertips and you can't eat any of it." She replied to his challenge defensively, saying, "Of course we may eat. It's only the fruit from the tree at the center of the garden that we are not to eat." She was already playing into Satan's scheme by even discussing God's orders with him. This was her first mistake—using poor judgment and failing to use God's courage in her dealings with him. She did not realize that her human-level courage was insufficient for the situation.

Consequently, she listened further as he appealed to her ego and her appetite. The fruit *did* look appealing. When he promised her the same ability as God to distinguish good from evil, she succumbed. He knew the right buttons to push to get a negative reaction. She then ate the forbidden fruit and gave some to Adam, changing the course of mankind forever.

When God confronted Eve as to her disobedience, the direct result of her impetuous choice, she could not shoulder the responsibility. Rather, she insisted that the snake *made* her disobey by tricking her.

How like our sister Eve we are. We have tendencies that cause us to react the same way she did. Yet just as the Lord God mercifully made garments to cover Eve's embarrassment, He knows what we need. Even when we forego God-given courage and give in to poor judgment, He lovingly brings restoration, if we give Him permission.

Confident Hope

One of the definitions of trust is "confident hope." What a beautiful dimension in our relationship with the Lord, to be surrounded by His confident hope.

In Psalm 125:2 we read, "Just as the mountains surround and protect Jerusalem, so the Lord surrounds and protects his people." How exciting to know that we fall heir to His protection when we fully trust Him.

First Samuel relates the story of Hannah, one of two wives of a man named Elkanah. His other wife had borne children, and poor barren Hannah found herself the brunt of ridicule by Peninnah—the "other woman." Her heart was broken as she cried day after day. Her husband didn't help the situation any by asking, "Isn't having me better than having 10 sons?"

Once when Hannah was praying in the tabernacle, Eli the priest thought she was drunk and told her to throw away her bottle. Even the preacher misunderstood her! Yet Hannah did not react angrily to any of the people who treated her unfairly. Instead her trust in the Lord remained steadfast. She even promised to give Him back her son if He chose to bless her with one.

The Lord graciously allowed her to become pregnant and she kept her promise. She took little Samuel to the

Tabernacle to be raised by Eli the priest. Eli had done a terrible job of raising his own sons so Hannah could have protested and reneged on her promise to God. Her trust was so complete, however, that she stated, "For all the earth is the Lord's and he has set the world in order. He will protect his godly ones..." (1 Samuel 2:8,9).

Because of Hannah's trusting attitude and lack of fear of the future, her only son became a mighty man of godly influence. Trusting in God by completely relying on His courage and not our own is always rewarded with His continual concern and protection.

Steps to Becoming a Courageous Woman

1. Ask the Lord to show you areas where you may be making a poor judgment.

2. Begin making a list of all the Scripture verses you can locate containing the word "trust."

3. Read Hannah's entire prayer of thanksgiving to the Lord in 1 Samuel 2:1-10.

4. Write your personal prayer of trust and thanksgiving to the Lord. Keep it to refer back to in times of discouragement.

5. Memorize Psalm 125:1,2.

> *Take responsibility for negative*
> *circumstances that are the result of*
> *poor judgment on your part.*

Realize that through God's power, you don't have to let circumstances defeat you physically, emotionally or spiritually.

A man's courage can sustain his broken body, but when courage dies, what hope is left?
—Proverbs 18:14

5

Dealing with Defeat

In the previous chapter, we looked at the various responses of Delores, Eve and Hannah during periods of temptation. We saw the disastrous results of relying on human rather than spiritual resources for courage. We also noted how these women's actions not only affected themselves, but other members of their families as well.

Hannah lived out her days filled with joy and thankfulness to a God she could gain courage from while Delores, who relied on her own strength, lives unhappily, merely existing. Eve lost her beautiful home and her loving, pure relationship with Adam and with God. Because she didn't trust God for His courage, she took matters into her own hands. Doubt and skepticism replaced trust, giving birth to fear.

It is interesting that the first time fear was mentioned in the Bible was immediately following the account of Eve's failure to use God-given courage to resist temptation. Studies show that fear directly affects us physically as well as mentally. Remember the nightmares I experienced during pregnancy, related in Chapter 1? They were caused by fear, but resulted in physical manifestations: lack of proper rest, nervousness, loss of appetite and extreme irritability. Fear often causes sweaty palms, upset stomach, shaky legs and a flushed feeling.

Are your circumstances defeating you physically?
Emotionally? Spiritually?

Failure to ask for God-given courage, coupled with fear, may genuinely harm your health. Your blood pressure may rise, the digestive system may not function properly or you may feel chronic fatigue. You may feel as though the daily routine is a continuous drag. The only consolation is that you are certainly not alone in those feelings. Eventually, however, you will need to deal with the cause. You may be surprised to find that fear of the known and unknown can account for that heavy, oppressive, feeling.

God-given Courage in Action

The opening Bible verse to this chapter describes one of the primary benefits of God-given courage—strength in times of broken health. I have observed this to be true in the life of my brother, Vernon. He is one of the most wonderful brothers anyone could ever ask for. Tall, handsome, outgoing, friendly, great father, super husband. For the past six years, however, he has been afflicted with Amyotrophic Lateral Sclerosis (A.L.S.), commonly known as Lou Gehrig's Disease.

A policeman for many years, his capacity for love and communication was used eventually as a liaison in the schools between the children and the police department. There could not have been a better spokesman to give the students a positive impression of those who uphold the law.

During a required training seminar, he seriously injured his shoulder while diving under a table in a make-shift obstacle course. He underwent two major surgeries to repair the damage, but experienced continual pain and weakness in his right arm. He tried to return to work from time to time, but because he was unable to quickly and strongly respond in case of physical attack, he could no longer wear the uniform of the occupation he loved.

He had enjoyed providing for his family, allowing his wife to stay home to care for their four children. The day came, unfortunately, when his disability pension could not support them so Donna went to work. They thought they had used up their allotment of courage in reversing roles—a drastic change in lifestyle—but their future would require more.

They had no inkling that a short time later the doctors would find the progressive degeneration of the muscles in Vernon's arms and shoulders was due to a dreaded, terminal disease, not the surgeries. Denial, anger, frustration and much questioning were the reactions of all who loved him.

He was such a godly man. He had graduated from Bible school, was serving as Sunday school director of a large church and always endeavored to raise his offspring in the "nurture and admonition" of the Lord. Was this how he was going to be rewarded when, earthly speaking, he should have lived an average of 30 more years?

We read everything we could find on A.L.S. and it was all bad news. No known cause and no cure.

It is hard for any of us who have never suffered a progressive, deadly illness to begin to know the emotional and mental processes that take place. After observing him closely over the past six years, however, I have learned much about fear versus courage.

In the beginning stages of his illness, Vernon continued his long distance running. In his final marathon he crossed the finish line long after an elderly woman had finished, but what mattered was that with the assistance and encouragement of his family, he did it! He knew his body's muscular structure was slowly but surely failing, and he wanted to run that one last race to assist the Muscular Dystrophy Association in its fund raising.

Refusing to Accept Defeat

After my husband Rich and I spent two weeks with Vernon and his equally courageous wife on a vacation last year, I began to understand more fully the faithfulness of God in supplying courage and Vern's "secrets" in not allowing his circumstances to defeat him. Even though he can no longer dress himself, feed himself, turn the pages of his Bible, go to the bathroom alone or scratch his nose, he always has an encouraging word for everyone. What characteristics would his kind of helplessness produce in us? Our ego would most assuredly take a beating. But he accepts assistance and is grateful for his devoted wife and others who feed him, whether at home or in a restaurant, and take care of his other needs. An electric wheelchair provides more mobility now, and this fall he enjoyed racing up and down the sidelines during his son's football games.

Vern's situation could drive him to depression or an irritable personality, but instead he is loved and admired by everyone who knows him. The doctors, nurses, fellow church members, neighbors and police co-workers all know he's found some sort of secret for coping, the same secret learned by all who have struggled with difficulty and survived with supernatural courage.

So, what's Vern's "secret"? Okay, everyone—here it is! He has learned, through prayer and God's Word, to focus his mind on things above and not on his condition. Over the years, he has disciplined his mind and heart so that no matter the circumstances, he has been able to give total adoration to his Lord and trust in Him completely. He has refused to let bitterness or self-pity overcome his God-given courage.

His future, in spite of the disease's progression, is filled with hope because of God's courage flowing through him. This does not mean he exists in a Pollyanna state or a constant attitude of denial. On the contrary, he is preparing for his eventual, complete paralysis. He knows he will most likely lose his ability to speak, which is already apparent. He knows and is preparing Donna and the family for his separation from them by death, barring a miracle. So you see, he is residing in a state of reality, not in defeat or fear.

Vernon is what God-given courage is about—making a deliberate choice to trust the Lord to infuse His Word and Spirit constantly into his life and provide the necessary courage. This is a specific, conscious decision on his part. Knowing that the Lord's courage is always available is an important aspect of his day to day battles. He is not willing to wave the white flag of surrender to the Enemy.

Persistence Pays

In Mark 7 there is the account of a courageous woman who, like Vernon, would not accept defeat. She was heartbroken because her little girl was possessed by a demon. In fact the evil spirit had complete control of her child. What a terrible feeling of helplessness for a parent. She could have said to herself, "Well, because I'm just a despised Gentile I'm not worthy to expect anything better. I'm hated by many of my neighbors. In fact, I'm probably just getting what I deserve."

Instead, she heard of someone named Jesus and traveled to seek His help. When she met the One she had heard so much about she instantly sensed His care for her, and He was possibly the last hope for her precious daughter. Her first act upon meeting him was to fall at His feet. What an important posture to be in, if not actually physically, then surely spiritually. To bow in complete submission to His ability to meet her need was important.

Jesus' reaction was disturbing at first, but I believe He was testing her sincerity for the purpose of strengthening her resolve. Jesus told her that He should help His own family first—the Jews. He made it clear He knew she was a Gentile. In fact, in His next breath He said, "It isn't right to take the children's food and throw it to the dogs."

About that time, I think I would have felt so humiliated and insulted I probably would have simply crawled away. Not this woman! She had such determination that she answered Jesus with a diplomatic and nonargumentative statement, "That's true, Sir, but even the puppies under the table are given some scraps from the children's plates." She was willing to release her own ego and admit that without His "throwing her some scraps" she would remain "hungry" and in need of healing for her daughter.

So, too, when we need His help we must come to the same place, humbly admitting to being totally inadequate in our own strength. The only way Vernon is able to clutch God's portion of courage is to admit his need and surrender his personal dreams and desires.

Because of her right attitude, Jesus honored the woman's plea for help. He told her that she had indicated a correct, contrite spirit and because of that, her daughter was at that moment totally healed of the demon's control. She ran home to find the little girl resting quietly in her bed.

Persistence, surrendering our pride, and admitting to being helpless without Divine assistance allows the Lord to override our circumstances and gives Him the opportunity to bestow His strength and courage on us. This requires an act of our will and is an ongoing process.

We meet new challenges daily, some greater than others. We find ourselves having to fight new battles constantly. As we submit our lives and circumstances to His ability to handle them from the start, there will be no need to accept defeat physically, emotionally or spiritually.

Steps to Becoming a Courageous Woman

1. List the areas of your life in which you are allowing the Enemy to bring defeat.

2. Ask the Lord to show you the specific steps you need to take to gain victory over your circumstances. Share these with a friend.

3. Read Mark 7:24-30 and draw any parallels between the woman's situation and yours.

4. Memorize Proverbs 18:14.

> *Realize that through God's power, you don't have to let circumstances defeat you physically, emotionally or spiritually.*

***The Lord* always
*hears your prayers, in spite
of how you may feel.***

*I'm not asking you to take them out of the world,
but to keep them safe from Satan's power.*
Prayer of Jesus—John 17:15

6

Where Is God When I Need Him?

In the preceding verse, John 17:15, Christ was praying for us—you and me! It's overwhelming to know that our Savior and Lord continually intercedes for us before the throne of God. Just as the mother in the previous chapter interceded for her demon-possessed daughter, so too does Christ act as our advocate.

Occasionally I act as my husband's assistant during trials when he performs the tasks of an attorney. (He also is a judge.) It is fascinating to follow the logical progression of his arguments and cross-examination as he builds the case for his client. In spite of my opinion that he does such a good job that he should win every case, he loses once in a while.

But Christ never loses a case. He has earned the authority and the blessing of Almighty God by His obedience even unto death. Because He went through His Gethsemane, He can enable us through ours.

Remember what Jesus cried out on the cross? " 'Eli, Eli, lama sabachthani,' which means, 'My God, my God, why have you forsaken me?' " (Matthew 27:46). He felt the silence and it must have disturbed Him.

*Do you ever feel as though God
is answering your requests with total silence?*

Perhaps you have also experienced times of feeling totally abandoned or ignored by God, exemplified by the vacuum-like silence that accompanies your prayers. You are not alone. Charlene, whose baby died in her arms, told me, "At that moment I felt I was in hell. I thought my prayers were not going above the ceiling."

Miree, with her husband and two small children, left her native land of Australia to minister in America. As the ship pulled away from the dock, she said, "I looked around at all our loved ones, both family and friends, and wondered which ones would be missing when we returned home. It all seemed like a step of foolishness at that moment." She did not feel God near her, even though she was following His will.

Barb was informed by the doctor one day that her 11-year-old daughter Angie had cancer. She described her feelings, "As I looked outside, the once sunny skies had grown dark with heavy black clouds and one of those summer downpours started. It was as if Heaven was releasing a flood of tears. I, too, began crying with deep sobbing as this was the most devastating news I had ever been given. I was an emotional wreck."

Angie shares that, "During the time that I was diagnosed as having cancer, I was having a hard time praying to God. Sometimes when I would pray, I would ask God why He did this to me. There were a lot of times I could not pray because I was mad at God."

Marlene, who has battled a disease commonly known as Lupus for approximately 27 years, has on many occasions come close to death. She says that at times she has felt forsaken by God and has questioned the pain and suffering she has endured.

Carolyn, shortly after losing her husband, father, brother-in-law and a close friend's husband in an airplane crash, admitted that "fear came in huge waves. How could I begin to cope? Suddenly, I felt responsible for so many people—my mother, my sister, my friend, 10 fatherless children, Ron's business, the farm—my fear was approaching panic."

Denise experienced walking through the Valley of the Shadow of Death with her beloved mother who fought cancer valiantly but lost. When Denise first heard the diagnosis she was devastated. "When I began to see her suffer I questioned the Lord daily. Why? Why? This was not what she deserved."

To be filled with doubt, fear, anger, frustration, horror and sorrow are natural human responses. To feel completely lacking in courage at times should not produce self-condemnation or guilt. The problems, however, become compounded and totally defeating when we stay in the throes of grief and distress.

I purposely shared these testimonies because they involve women with whom I am well-acquainted. Over the years, as dire circumstances have been thrust upon them, I have watched each one become more and more effective for Christ and His Kingdom. After observing these and other women who have faced what seemed like insurmountable situations, I have come to the conclusion that in order for any of us to be effective for our Lord, we have to die to self.

Paul says it profoundly when he writes:

> When you put a seed into the ground it doesn't grow into a plant unless it "dies" first. And when the green shoots come up out of the seed, it is very different from the seed you first planted. For all you put into the ground is a dry little seed of

wheat, or whatever it is you are planting, then God gives it a beautiful new body—just the kind he wants it to have; a different kind of plant grows from each kind of seed (1 Corinthians 15:36-38).

Each of my friends' experience was unique and the Lord has produced fruit through each life in His extraordinary ways. As each woman faced her own spiritual death, recognizing her inability to face the crisis, her Savior supplied the same courage God had granted to Him in Gethsemane.

During one of many sleepless nights, Charlene cried out, "God, I can't go on like this, I am going to lose my mind." She tells, "The Holy Spirit, at that moment, impressed on me that He was there to comfort me but just as I had received salvation, I had to choose to receive His comfort. I realized that night that I could will to fall apart, I could will to have a nervous breakdown, making me ineffective as a wife and mother, or I could choose to allow the Holy Spirit to comfort and strengthen me through this horrible experience. Since then, God has proven His faithfulness in many ways. I have discovered that faithfulness is His very character."

The morning Miree and her family left their home in Melbourne, she went to her cabin on board the ship. She read the Scripture verse on the calendar for the day that she had torn off the wall prior to leaving home. As she read it, her heart skipped a beat with excitement. She declares, "God cared enough for me to speak a promise, a confirmation as solid as a rock.

"The Bible verses for the day were Mark 10:29,30, 'There is no man (or woman) that has left house, or brethren, or sisters, or father, or mother, or wife, or children, or lands for My sake and the Gospel's, but he shall receive an hundred-fold now in this time, and in the age to come, eternal life.'

"What more did we need? God's call and now God's promise. Somehow the sadness and loneliness, the fear of the unknown, the struggle and uncertainty of a new begin-ning in a different culture with two small children, all seemed to disappear with the overwhelming peace in knowing we were obeying God."

Barb and Angie bear witness to the special work that the Lord accomplished in their lives. Barb remembers, "Our family bonds were strengthened; our faith in God grew as we watched His faithfulness. We became more compas-sionate toward others, but I also had to continually deal with strong feelings of resentment. It did not seem fair to have our beautiful daughter, Angie, stricken with this dreaded disease.

"One day I realized that God did not owe me anything. Jesus had already done so much for us. I finally came to the place where I could say, 'God, I do not ask for a reason, you do not owe me one, and I have no complaints with you. In spite of everything, I choose to live to glorify you.' "

Angie is free of cancer today, 9 years later, a miracle of the grace of God. She adds this postscript, "Even though I was mad at God when I was sick, I kept faith in Him. He gave me many great friends who gave me the support I needed."

Marlene is still struggling with Lupus but says, "We do not always understand why things happen as they do, but He has asked us to trust Him and He will provide the strength and courage needed to face tomorrow. God's Word has become as important to me as breathing. Often He has spoken to me so clearly through Scriptures. One such passage is 2 Corinthians 1:3-5:

> What a wonderful God we have—he is the Father of our Lord Jesus Christ, the source of every mercy, and the one who so wonderfully comforts and strengthens us in our hardships and trials. And why does he do this? So that when others are troubled, needing our sympathy and encouragement, we can pass on to them this same help and comfort God has given us. You can

be sure that the more we undergo sufferings for Christ, the more he will shower us with his comfort and encouragement.

"Each time I read God's Word, I can feel the Lord's eternal love surround me. His strength, not mine, has been sufficient!"

Carolyn, who was beset by fear after the death of her husband, remembers the night she sobbed into her pillow and cried, "Jesus, I can't face this alone. I need your help. Please give me strength for the days and nights ahead, and above all, if you do nothing else, please, please release me from fear." She says, "I can honestly say that the fear left me and in its place, came peace. I relaxed and slept and have not spent a fearful night since. That is not to say that I have not faced huge problems, but the fear of the unknown left. The Lord invaded me with His courage."

In her healing process, Carolyn also relied heavily on God's Word and His promises. She began underlining promises with bright orange ink and now as she looks back over them, she can clearly see how God was speaking comfort to her in her raging storm.

Denise found that during her much-loved mother's year of suffering with cancer it was a constant struggle for her to know how to pray. She says, "Sometimes I would simply plead, 'O, God, show me how I should pray.' How patient, faithful, and comforting He always was in those times of uncertainty. Often I found myself only capable of calling the name of Jesus over and over. He was constantly nearby to help me.

"My mother's life spoke to me of God's faithfulness many times during her illness. The meaning of Philippians 4:7 became apparent as I watched her reaction to the mounting difficulties. It says, 'And the peace of God, which passeth all understanding, shall keep your hearts and minds through Christ Jesus' (KJV). It has become a great comfort to me to know that Christ measures peace and strength according to our needs.

"I can no longer sit and question, 'Why wasn't she healed?' or 'Why did she have to die?' The answer lies in the fact that so much has been accomplished for Christ and for eternity through her death that I am beginning to understand God's plan just a little. He does make all things beautiful in His time. I thank Him for that!"

Jesus went through His Gethsemane with the same human emotions that we experience when we go through ours. Paul Billheimer expressed Christ's struggle when he wrote:

> The battle which continued through His ministry reached an incredible intensity in the Garden. The demonic and satanic pressure upon His spirit was so unutterably devastating that it brought Jesus to the very brink of death. He cried, "My soul is exceeding sorrowful, even unto death" (Matthew 26:38), while from His tortured face the blood drops oozed and spattered onto the ground. The mind staggers and human language bankrupts itself in attempting to describe this scene. As God, He could have called a multitude of angels to His aid, but had He done so He would not have suffered only as a man.[2]

The more I study the struggle that Jesus went through as He faced the most difficult circumstances in His life, the more clearly I see how He is able to identify with us. His God-Man wills were in total conflict. His "Humanness" wanted to avoid at all costs the pain and suffering that He knew were ahead, while His "Godness" recognized the necessity of it all.

The dilemma He faced was that in order to be completely obedient to the Father's will, He had to deny His own. The apostle Paul records this struggle in Hebrews, "Yet while Christ was here on earth he pleaded with God, praying with tears and agony of soul to the only one who would save him from [premature] death. And God heard his prayers because of his strong desire to obey God at all times. And even though Jesus was God's Son, he had to learn from experience what it was like to obey, when obeying meant suffering" (Hebrews 5:7,8).

To question, cry, appeal and protest is not wrong. Wrong occurs if our walk with Christ is put on hold or our protests turn to rebellion.

By faith, know that when you place "a call," a prayer, to your Heavenly Father, the answer is on the way—His *perfect* answer. With His answer, because his Son paid the price, comes courage.

Steps to Becoming a Courageous Woman

1. Are you currently facing a difficult time in your life?

2. Do you feel as though God has abandoned you?

3. Write a letter to God expressing your feelings.

4. Read John 17, making note of Christ's prayers for you.

5. Memorize John 17:15, remembering that God, the Father, heard Jesus, the Son's, prayer.

The Lord always hears your prayers, in spite of how you may feel.

***Always be certain
you are listening to the
right voices.***

*Be of good courage, and he shall strengthen
your heart, all ye that hope in the Lord.*
—Psalm 31:24 KJV

7

Hearing His Voice: Loud and Clear

In the previous chapter, I explored the honest, transparent reactions to difficult circumstances experienced by seven women I know personally, as well as Christ's response when He faced betrayal and death. Initially, each reacted with dismay and questioning. However, these individuals did not remain immobilized or conquered by events. Instead they sought the Lord's courage by entering and delighting in His presence. It was imperative that they listened to His voice directing them through His Word and Spirit, or the results could have been disastrous.

Are you listening to the right "voices"?

Every day there are distractions that come along in our lives to entice us from the path the Lord wants us to take. Our society is in a constant state of change and it expects

73

us to keep changing with it. At times the change is good, but often it is detrimental to Christians.

The Importance of Motherhood

For instance, the pressure placed on mothers today to be fullfilled and productive *outside* the home is immense. The children of parents of the 1960s are becoming parents themselves. The prevalent idea put forth by society in the '60s was that traditional roles had not worked so let's try something different. Many solid, traditional values were derided in books, magazines, on television, by educators and even by some theologians. As I said previously, some of the changes have been positive. Yet the change that has had the most far-reaching ramifications and the one that has affected millions, adversely I believe, has been to encourage mothers to get out of the home and into the workplace.

I'll admit that for economic reasons when Rich was still in school I worked outside the home to contribute the greater share of our support. I also worked during law school and until Rich began his legal practice, taking time off occasionally to give birth. I felt guilty for leaving our children, but I also felt extreme financial pressure.

Gradually the Lord began to show me what we could do without and corners we could cut to save enough money so I could stay home with the children. Conflicts and questions plagued my thinking. Wouldn't I vegetate being with children all the time? How would I be able to use my God-given gifts to the fullest? Remember this was in the '60s and the pressure was on. Just a housewife and mother? How very ordinary. Sounded so unglamourous and unworthwhile.

As I looked at our old green hand-me-down couch with its innards becoming "outards," I felt the pull many times to earn extra money as a secretary. On the days when the kids were anything but cooperative with one another, let alone with me, I would feel the tug to hire a sitter to put up with all their "garbage." I was too great to waste away doing such unimportant tasks as changing dirty diapers, wiping runny noses, disciplining fighting youngsters, mopping floors, scrubbing toilets and a thousand other humdrum jobs. Wasn't I? But what of my precious family?

One day during my devotions, I read in Psalms the words, "O Lord, you alone are my hope; I've trusted you from childhood. Yes, you have been with me from birth and have helped me constantly—no wonder I am always praising you! My success—at which so many stand amazed—is because you are my mighty protector" (Psalm 71:5-7).

This portion of Scripture was like an inoculation of courage to me. I knew I was being obedient to God's will and I knew it was for my family's well-being that I stay home, but this prayer of David's gave me a new desire to be the wife and mother He wanted me to be. Yes, it did require that I accept His courage many days when discouragement, "cabin-fever," or financial strain became wearing on me. Now that our children have become parents themselves, I notice that they are working through the same pressures I did.

I realize God has a unique plan for every life so please don't read condemnation into my testimony if you are working. I would ask of you, though, to allow His voice to come through loud and clear as to His perfect will for you and your family.

If it's success you're after, He'll give it to you in surprising ways. I'm convinced being a mom is the most important job in the world. Investing time, energy and creativity in little lives of "wet cement," as author Anne Ortland calls them, will reap eternal as well as temporal dividends.

The pressure for monetary gain is very strong in our society. "Outside" voices are always beckoning us to purchase a new item that will greatly enhance our life, from toothpaste to a new house. If obtaining possessions becomes our primary goal, to the exclusion of listening for the Lord's direction, we will often miss His perfect will.

If you have financial needs and you know God is calling you to stay home, ask Him to show you areas in which you can conserve and possible ways to supplement your income while remaining with the children. Be prepared to ask for daily doses of courage from the Lord to meet the challenges and opportunities of full-time motherhood.

Remaining Sensitive to the Father's Voice

Our grandson Matthew was born three months premature on October 4, 1987. As he struggled to live, attached to several different machines which sustained his tiny life, Rich and I and our son Kendall (Matthew's daddy) would gather around his isolette. His mother Caela was too ill to visit him for a few days. We quickly received a crash course from the doctors and nurses as to what the readings on various monitors meant. We soon learned what were "good" signs and what were "bad."

During one of our visits on the second day of Matthew's life, I made a remarkable discovery. Although he weighed only a little over two pounds, was 14 inches long and labored to breathe with the aid of a respirator, he taught me a valuable lesson.

As we stood there, praying and talking, I noticed that whenever Kendall spoke, the numbers on Matthew's monitors would improve. His oxygen saturation level and his heart rate would look better. I heard the nurse tell Kendall to talk to and spend as much time at Matthew's miniature bedside as possible because he would do much better when his daddy was there.

I asked her if that was why we noticed positive signs on his charts when Kendall was there and she said that, yes, he did indeed know his father's voice. He was familiar with it from hearing it while still in the womb. Amazing! Out of all the voices and sounds he heard in the neonatal intensive care unit, he could pick out his daddy's.

What a lesson concerning hearing and discerning our Heavenly Father's voice. Of all the sounds we hear coming from the world around us, we must pick up His voice even if it comes in the form of a whisper to our heart. We'll know without any doubt that we've heard from Him.

A Woman with Acute Hearing

Jochebed was a real woman who lived in Old Testament times amid dreadful circumstances who still had proper sensitivity to God's voice. She was so alert to His calling that even though she was due to give birth to a son whose death sentence had already been ordered, she listened to instruction from the Lord as to the importance of preserving her son's life. At His direction, she did everything possible to hide her son from the authorities so his murder could not be carried out. Every boy born during that time period was to be thrown into the river.

At the Lord's direction she carefully fashioned a basket out of bulrushes and plugged the holes with pitch. Then she laid her precious 3-month-old son into the basket and placed it in the river. About here I might have argued something like this: "But, Lord, I thought you wanted him saved alive! Can I please put him in that nice dry cave up yonder? Why the river? Babies can drown in inches of water. Please, God, not the river!"

Dear Jochebed apparently didn't even argue with the Lord. She simply obeyed. Her obedience to His instructions must have taken courage—hiding her son for the first three months of life and then entrusting him to the dangers of the river.

In case you do not remember the rest of the story, this precious boy was rescued from the river by the beautiful daughter of Pharaoh. She recognized him immediately as one of the babies whose death sentence was imposed by her father.

The Bible says that he was a "goodly child," but I like to think that perhaps just as the princess saw him for the first time, an angel pinched little Moses a tiny bit and he began to cry. This brought a compassionate response from her and she loved him and felt protective immediately.

Possessing a mother's concern and curiosity, Jochebed had her older daughter keep a watchful eye on the basket and its cargo from the riverbank. So while Pharaoh's daughter was contemplating her new-found responsibility, Miriam quickly asked if she needed someone to nurse and help raise the child. Of course she did, so Miriam ran and summoned Jochebed.

The Importance of Obedience

The daughter of the ruler who ordered this baby's death entrusted him back into the keeping of his own mother. Could the princess have known? We're not told, but we do know that Jochebed was paid wages for nursing and raising her own son for, according to some Bible scholars, possibly up to 12 years. And who paid those wages? Why, of course, the Pharaoh who had ordered his death. How beautiful and perfect the plan of God! Was it an easy one to follow? I'm certain that it was not, but the future of an entire nation pivoted on Jochebed's obedience.

Moses, whose name means "drawn from the water," became a mighty instrument in God's hand. If not for his mother's obedience, the Lord's ultimate plan could not have been carried out.

There will be times in your life when after hearing His voice, you would rather tune it out or ignore what He is saying to you. There were times when my children were young, if they thought I was calling them to run an errand or do a chore, they acted stone deaf. If I called them to the telephone or for a piece of cake, they came running.

How like children we are in our behavior toward our Heavenly Father's voice. If we are to be used for His glory in carrying out His perfect plan, not only for ourselves but for our loved ones as well, we must first discern which voice is His. Only by spending time in His presence and listening to His Spirit will we be able to recognize His voice as He speaks courage to our lives. When we quietly listen with our hearts, we will gain new strength to carry out our convictions and new resolve to follow His direction. Jochebed was able to courageously carry out God's will because she knew His voice and unwavering faithfulness from firsthand experience.

Steps to Becoming a Courageous Woman

1. Read Exodus 1 and 2 and list the ways Jochebed was obedient.

2. Note the times the Lord was faithful in the same chapters.

3. Spend quiet time in the Lord's presence today, listening to Him speak to you.

4. Ask Him for wisdom and discernment regarding any decisions you may be facing.

5. Memorize Psalm 31:24 and claim its promise.

Always be certain you are
listening to the right voices.

***Always remember
the Lord's promises
and capabilities
are more than adequate.***

*Your steadfast love, O Lord, is as great as all the
heavens. Your faithfulness reaches beyond the
clouds.*
                                        —Psalm 36:5

8

Never-Changing Faithfulness

Mary Gay, a well-known speaker from Philadelphia, says that when she goes through difficulties she discovers a lot about herself and a whole lot more about God. She is a Christian who has experienced great depths of sorrow: extensive hospitalization throughout her teens including the removal of a lung, the death of her first husband at a young age, the destruction of a son's mind through a hidden sprinkling of the drug PCP in his food, and other severe challenges. Her favorite saying is, "Jesus Christ is *alive!*" Now, how do you suppose she can make that claim so positively? She *knows* because she has experienced His faithfulness again and again. She is well-qualified to make that statement.

Occasionally I visit the courtroom over which my husband presides as a judge. He will not allow hearsay conversation or second-hand testimony to be introduced as evidence. It must be first-hand, first-person knowledge. The only way for us to know God's faithfulness and testify to it is to experience it for ourselves. If we never needed His faithfulness, we would take it for granted and would just be mouthing platitudes when comforting others.

Learning of His Faithfulness

One of my favorite hymns contains the following lines: "Pardon for sin and a peace that endureth, Thy own dear presence to cheer and to guide; Strength for today and bright hope for tomorrow, Blessings all mine, with ten thousand beside!" How often I have sung that song, "Great Is Thy Faithfulness," in the middle of chaotic circumstances. The reassurance of its words brings peace and confidence in His abiding attention to my needs.

Christ's faithfulness which strengthens our courage is displayed daily in many ways if we have the spiritual eyes with which to see it. Circumstances often become so overwhelming that our soul-vision becomes impaired or completely obscured. We envision ourselves to be beggarly, when we're heirs to the King of the universe. We believe ourselves to be almost annihilated by our Enemy, when our Captain has never been defeated in battle. There are times we feel absolutely worthless, yet He says that our soul's value is equal to the wealth of the entire world (Psalm 49:8,9).

> *Why do we act as though the Lord's promises and capabilities are inadequate?*

When we doubt His faithfulness, the foundation stone of our God-given courage begins to disintegrate. To doubt means to lack confidence in someone or something. Once it takes over where God is concerned, it becomes easy to deny His faithfulness.

How easily we forget promises such as, "No good *thing* will he withhold from them that walk uprightly" (Psalm 84:11 KJV), and "I will instruct you (says the Lord) and guide you along the best pathway for your life; I will advise you and watch your progress" (Psalm 32:8).

Just prior to physically departing the earth Christ said, "I am leaving you with a gift—peace of mind and heart! And the peace I give isn't fragile like the peace the world gives. So don't be troubled or *afraid*" (John 14:27, italics mine).

Experiencing His Faithfulness

My Grandmother Holden had a great sense of the Lord's presence and faithfulness. As a child, I remember her carrying on countless conversations with Him, often something like this, "Now, Lord, I've lost my glasses again but you know exactly where I put them. Lord, because you promised you'd take care of me and watch out for me, please help me find my glasses."

Invariably within minutes I'd hear her cry out, "Oh, here they are! Thank you, Lord, I knew you could do it." She had learned that He was faithful in the little needs of life. Personally, it's in the minuscule corners of my day that I love to discover the Lord's eye is on me.

When I first began to speak and minister before groups, I knew I needed to appear presentable. That required a nice dress, but how to get one out of our meager budget was the challenge. I would, from time to time, drop by one of the nicest dress shops in our city—just to look, mind you! I had been earnestly, but timidly praying for an attractive dress to wear for speaking. Would the Lord want to be bothered with such a trivial request when so many people had monumental needs?

One day a friend and I were browsing at the mall, waiting for our children to get out of school. We decided to survey the sales racks in this same classy store.

My eyes suddenly caught sight of a darling red, white and blue linen dress with the appropriate high collar and long sleeves. Just perfect but I could probably never afford it, I thought to myself. My hands found the price tag and incredulously I read $125 with a slash through it and progressive prices—$100, $75, $50, $30, finally stopping at $14. Fourteen dollars! "Do you suppose it will fit?" I asked my friend. Well it did, and I "just happened" to have enough money. This might seem like a trivial example, but it shows how much God does care about the details of our lives.

Doubting His Faithfulness

Loss of belief in God's faithfulness and capabilities produces great discouragement when it appears our situation is not improving and may even look like it's worsening. There was an Old Testament king whose reaction to his plight parallels many of ours. I'm thankful his story is recorded in Isaiah for our benefit.

"During the reign of Ahaz (the son of Jotham and grandson of Uzziah), Jerusalem was attacked by King Rezin of Syria and King Pekah of Israel (the son of Remaliah). But it was not taken; the city stood. However, when the news came to the royal court, 'Syria is allied with Israel against us!' the hearts of the king and his people trembled with fear as the trees of a forest shake in a storm. Then the Lord said to Isaiah, 'Go out to meet King Ahaz, you and Shear-jashub, your son. You will find him at the end of the aqueduct which leads from Gihon Spring to the upper reservoir, near the road that leads down to the bleaching field.

" 'Tell him to quit worrying,' the Lord said. 'Tell him he needn't be frightened by the fierce anger of those two has-beens, Rezin and Pekah. Yes, the kings of Syria and Israel are coming against you.... But the Lord God says, 'This plan will not succeed....' " (Isaiah 7:1-7).

The Lord gave assurance in the middle of troublesome times that He would give victory. As far as the Lord was concerned, He didn't even want Ahaz to worry about the formidable enemy he was facing. He called the two kings who were his foes, "has-beens." In God's plan for Ahaz and for Israel, they were already history. The problem arose when Ahaz refused to believe the Lord's promise. God knew Ahaz's heart and said, "You don't believe me? If you want me to protect you, you must learn to believe what I say" (Isaiah 7:9).

Don't you think this statement from the Lord Himself would have been enough of an incentive to believe in His faithfulness? Not so with Ahaz. The Lord challenged Ahaz to ask for a sign that God meant what He said concerning victory over the enemy. God left the field wide open when He told Ahaz to ask for anything in heaven and on earth. For me, that would have been an offer too good to refuse.

But Ahaz refused to ask the Lord for a sign, saying he didn't want to bother Him. What an excuse and how common—the ordinary, garden-variety human. What a missed opportunity to put God to the test and grow in knowledge of the Lord's faithfulness. What a great lesson and declaration it would have been to the entire nation of Israel.

For whatever reasons, perhaps pride or unbelief, Ahaz exhausted the Lord God's patience. In doing so, he caused the Lord to choose the sign and what a sign! It has remained through all the succeeding generations, a sign of victory. God named the sign "Immanuel," which means "God with us." God foretold that this Sign would be born of a virgin and would be one who would walk along with us.

He would be "God with us" as we give Him permission to be. Just as Ahaz elected to turn his back on the Lord's advice, we do the same thing when we regard Him as helpless or doubt His faithfulness. Victory is ours, but we must declare it!

Steps to Becoming a Courageous Woman

1. List the ways the Lord has been faithful to you today, the last week and the past month.

2. Is there a situation you are facing that has caused you to doubt God's faithfulness?

3. Write it down and present it to the Lord.

4. Pray and ask Him for a sign of His faithfulness.

5. Memorize Psalm 36:5 and recite it whenever you are troubled by circumstances.

Always remember
the Lord's promises
and capabilities
are more than adequate.

***Allow the Lord
to have control of
your situation and do not
tie His hands.***

*Don't be impatient. Wait for the Lord, and he
will come and save you! Be brave, stouthearted
and courageous. Yes, wait and he will help you.*
—Psalm 27:14

9

Tying the Lord's Hands with Man-Made Solutions

———

The disbelief demonstrated by King Ahaz eventually resulted not only in his own spiritual collapse, but that of his followers as well. In 2 Chronicles 28:19 we read, "He (Ahaz) had destroyed the spiritual fiber of Judah and had been faithless to the Lord." He began to offer sacrifices to the gods of the kings of Syria who defeated him.

Ahaz's thinking became so convoluted that he believed the pagan gods must have been stronger and more powerful than his God. As a result, he chose to join their ranks. He went even further and nailed the doors of the Temple shut to prevent others from worshiping the one true God.

King Ahaz's willful faithlessness led to his ruin and that of all his people. What a sorry, disobedient man, you might be saying. Let me, however, draw some parallels.

Are you allowing the Lord to have control or are you tying His hands?

Compromise and succumbing to circumstances was easier and easier as King Ahaz's doubt became dominant.

Man-made solutions became the preferred choice.

We, too, often feel there is no answer to our situation. We say, "God you can't pull it off this time; it's too messy even for you." In doing so, we tie His hands to act on our behalf.

Some of the current human solutions to serious problems include: abortion, divorce, and choosing to use drugs or alcohol to escape reality. And as our society becomes more permissive, behavior that was frowned upon in times past is often condoned. Even Christians' boundaries of right and wrong are becoming more and more ambiguous.

Pressure of Our Society

If you don't think our rules of behavior have changed all that much, watch any of the current talk shows on television. The morals and ethics discussed and approved of are, for the most part, startling. They often reveal a blatant disobedience to godly principles as the guests tell the world of their man-made solutions to life's needs.

As Christians we turn the television off in disgust and we piously thank God we're not like that. But aren't we? Have you never reacted rashly to solve a problem simply on an emotional level? I confess that I have on many occasions. Sometimes the results have only hurt me. At other times, my actions have affected my loved ones, friends, co-workers and even other Believers.

Patience has never been one of my virtues and often I seek quick solutions to sticky problems. I say or do things strictly on an emotional level, like the time I gave one of our daughters an ultimatum. She was dating a young man of whom both my husband and I strongly disapproved. Instead of allowing the Lord to work it out, we told her if she continued to date him, she would have to leave school and come home.

We thought that would solve the problem, but instead it

drove their dating "underground" and forced their relationship closer. If we had not tied the Lord's hands by taking matters into our own, I'm certain He would have worked out a better solution. But I couldn't wait for that to happen. Rich and I had even committed our beautiful daughter to the Lord again but was that enough? No, we still took the situation into our hands and reacted out of human emotion. A few months later, God did solve what for us was a difficult problem, but we undoubtedly delayed the solution.

Alan Redpath wrote some sound advice in his book *The Making of a Man of God*:

> Never act in a panic. Never act when your emotions are aroused and your blood is at the boiling point. Wait until your blood begins to beat steadily again. If at any moment of tremendous pressure you feel that you *must* do something, that moment is the time when you will be apt to make the most tragic mistake in judgment.[3]

How correct he is! It is so hard to wait for the Lord to act, especially if you are a "Type A" personality like me. If I see a wrong, I want to correct it immediately.

When our kids were teenagers, I remember trying to play Holy Spirit in their lives on more than one occasion. Did it work? Oh, they might have "shaped up" for a while, but because Christ didn't do the work, it was short-lived.

Pressure Forces Impatience

Psalm 27:14, as quoted on page 89, has become one of my most often-quoted Scriptures because of the strength its promise holds. However, there is a condition placed on the Lord's ability to help us. It's that little four letter word—wait. If we are obedient and do as the verse says, then He is able to do as He promises, to help. We are also admonished to be brave, stouthearted and courageous. In other words, we are to resolve to react by *not* reacting, first and foremost, on an emotional level.

Imagine yourself late for a meeting and you are driving rapidly (not breaking the speed limit, you understand!) but you are in a definite hurry. Suddenly up ahead you hear the clanging of a loud bell. Lights begin to flash and you see the gates lowered as your way is blocked by the 7 o'clock train.

What are your alternatives? Basically there are three. First, you could choose to make a U turn and try to get to your destination by another route. Second, you could be foolish and not pay any attention to the warning signs. There would, however, be a high price to pay. What meeting could be that important? The third alternative would be to wait for the train to pass before you safely continued on to your destination.

We have the same three choices regarding any challenge we face. We can try to manipulate people and circumstances, we can plunge full steam ahead and strew wreckage along the way, or we can *wait* for the Lord to open the road.

Pressure for Decisions

My sister-in-law Reni has known a lifetime of waiting upon the Lord for each day's breath. She was born with a heart condition with the eloquent name of "Corrected Transposition with Ventricle Septal Defect and Pulmonary Stenosis." All of that means her heart is in backwards and her blood flows the opposite way throughout her body.

Once while her husband Glen was stationed in Germany as an Army Chaplain, her condition worsened. She developed an irregular heartbeat and began experiencing severe dizzy spells. On the advice of her doctor, they boarded a medical evacuation flight to Walter Reed Hospital.

The medical experts there came to the conclusion that open heart surgery would not do any good, but that a pacemaker might help.

With the emphasis on the word "might," Reni had a monumental decision to make. There was a risk in implanting and then relying on a pacemaker. Was this the route the Lord desired they take? Up to that point, she had relied on Him totally for strength and sustaining of life.

After much prayer and searching for the one right answer, the Lord showed her a rather obscure verse in the Old Testament. It is found in Ezra 9:8, "And now for a little space grace hath been *shewed* from the LORD our God, to leave us a remnant to escape, and to give us a nail in his holy place, that our God may lighten our eyes, and give us a little reviving in our bondage" (KJV).

The meaning of the verse was vague to her initially, but slowly the Lord began to open her understanding. He wanted to be her nail to hold her fast. If a nail releases a picture or shelf it is holding up, those items will come crashing down. He promised Reni that as her nail, He would hold her securely and not let her down. He reminded her that it was nails that held His Son to the cross because Jesus honored what those nails were doing. He *allowed* them to hold Him.

Reni knew that she had to continue to wait on Him to be her Source and not yield to a man-made solution. That was a number of years ago, and she is still going strong.

Succumbing to Pressure

When David appeared as a boy before the giant Goliath he cried out, "You come to me with a sword and a spear, but I come to you in the name of the Lord of the armies of heaven and of Israel—the very God whom you have defied. And Israel will learn that the Lord does not depend on weapons to fulfill his plans—he works without regard to human means!" (1 Samuel 17:45,47).

He spoke these words, I'm certain, with great conviction yet four chapters later we see him behaving exactly the opposite. On one occasion he lied (1 Samuel 21:2) and on another he ate the holy bread from the Tabernacle (1 Samuel 21:6). A short time later, he took matters into his own hands and borrowed a heathen weapon, the sword of Goliath the Philistine whom he had killed (1 Samuel 21:8,9). Then he became afraid of the king who was harboring him and pretended to be insane. He went so far as to scratch on doors like an animal and let drool flow down his beard (1 Samuel 21:12). King Achish believed the ruse but don't you suppose for every man-made solution in the 21st chapter of Samuel, God had a better one?

I believe He did, but His hands were tied by David's own actions. Instead of waiting for Divine deliverance, David became fearful and succumbed to other avenues of behavior. He must have written Psalm 27:14 after this series of experiences when he learned the importance of not being impatient but waiting for the Lord to act. He learned the consequences of not being brave, stouthearted or courageous in the Lord.

My constant prayer is for God to bestow the attributes of *waiting on* and *trusting in* Him upon me, and that I will receive them. Is it your prayer too?

Steps to Becoming a Courageous Woman

1. Read Exodus chapters 17–21 and make two lists, one containing all the times the Lord delivered David. The other list should contain all the times that David devised man-made solutions.

2. Make a third list of areas of your life in which you have a need.

3. Beside each need write "L" signifying that you are allowing the Lord to work it out as you release it to Him.

4. Pray, requesting His attributes of bravery, stouthearted-
   ness and courage.

5. Memorize Psalm 27:14.

> ***Allow the Lord to have control***
> ***of your situation and do not tie***
> ***His hands.***

Determine not to live
in the fantasyland of
"if only."

The Lord's promise is sure. He speaks no careless word, all he says is purest truth, like silver seven times refined.

—Psalm 12:6

10

Living an "If Only" Existence

One would think that because David learned so many profound lessons in God's faithfulness compared to his human frailty he would never have failed again by acting on his own wisdom. David expressed his awe of the Lord when he said, "How great you are, Lord God! We have never heard of any other god like you. And there is no other god" (2 Samuel 7:22).

Yet just four chapters later we're told of his adulterous affair with Bathsheba, the wife of one of his officers. And did he ever use a man-made solution to try to patch up that situation! David had her husband Uriah murdered and then ordered others to lie concerning his death. I'm certain that the regret of his deeds followed him to his grave.

Do you live in a constant state of "if only"?

If David had the opportunity to do it over again, he probably would have lived his life differently. How often we have said that to ourselves. However, David would not have

101

known the depths of God's forgiveness, faithfulness and God-given courage were it not for those times of failure and restoration.

In Psalm 51, written shortly after the prophet Nathan confronted David concerning his crime, David implores the Lord not to keep looking at his sin but to restore his joy by erasing his failures. He also writes that more important than doing penance or offering a sacrifice is a contrite, broken heart. No more self-pride or haughtiness in coping with difficulties.

Let me interject that too often we blame Satan for the messes we get ourselves into. Remember Eve in the fourth chapter of this book? It's interesting that David was man enough to completely shoulder the responsibility for his actions. In the same Psalm, he talks about being conceived in sin and in verse 3, he admits his "shameful deed." In the following verse, he says, "It is against you and you alone I sinned, and did this terrible thing."

One of the most important principles for having godly courage is to admit that we have had a bad attitude and that we have been mistaken in our actions or reactions. We have to stop living in an "if only" world. We need to confess our deficiencies and stop using "if only" as an excuse for lack of courage.

"If only" I hadn't married old so-and-so; "if only" I hadn't had the parents I did; "if only" I hadn't been abused as a child; "if only" I had a better job. The list could go on and on. The "if only" syndrome postpones direct confrontation with our Lord and keeps us from receiving His help.

My husband Rich was a full-time college student during our first five years of marriage and I said "if only" constantly. We had three children by the time he graduated from law school and as I've already mentioned, we lived at or below poverty level. At least once a day for the entire five years, I thought or said aloud, "If only we had more money, then all our problems would be solved."

Later, as Rich's law practice grew and the children became older, I realized how wrong I was. Having fewer monetary worries was *not* the solution to all our problems. Our lives continued to be constantly challenged by difficulties and problems. I've learned we have to rely on and remain dependent on the Lord to be our Source in every area, not just our bank account.

Living Above Destructive Circumstances

Jean has continued over the years to be a godly example of a woman who has every right, humanly speaking, to live in an "if only" world. Her childhood was very difficult due to dysfunctional family patterns. She married while still in high school and within a few years gave birth to two daughters and one son. However, her marriage was doomed to failure from the start because of her husband's chosen lifestyle. Divorce seemed the only way out.

Six years later she renewed her vows of marriage with her former husband and bore another son. Another divorce. Another failure.

Her need for acceptance continually drove her to seek others' approval as her barometer for self-worth. Yet the harder she sought, the lower her esteem went. She had accepted Jesus as her Savior in fifth grade, but now as an adult she still wanted and needed people to tell her she was loved.

At a Christian camp one summer where she and her four children had sought a semblance of security, she began to realize how special she was to the Lord. Through prayer, counseling and being open to scriptural teaching she was gradually healed of destructive self-hatred and rejection. The Lord also gave her a love for her mother that she had not previously experienced. Her responsibilities remained monumental, however, with four children to raise as a single parent.

After years of struggling to survive financially, she took a courageous step of faith and began depending solely on her job, not welfare, to support her family. The past few years have not been easy financially, physically, emotionally or spiritually. She recently lost a godly second husband to cancer after being married only a few months. But throughout the years I have known her, Jean has not blamed God or become bitter.

She is like David in that respect for in joy and in sorrow, in poverty and prosperity, she has had a heart after God. Even though her dreams have been shattered time and again, her faith in God has remained steady.

In a small yet powerful book, *Destined for the Throne*, Paul E. Billheimer writes:

> A God who can take all "evil," even the mistakes and sins of a penitent child of God, and by the alchemy of His divine grace so transform them that they boomerang against Satan, enhance the character of the saint, and redound to the glory of God, is worthy of unceasing praise. A God with such a character is adequate basis for obedience to the exhortation, "Giving thanks always for all things in the name of our Lord Jesus Christ to God, even the Father" (Ephesians 5:20 ASV).[4]

Living in Thanks in Order to Trust

To give thanks in the middle of our broken dreams or disappointments is a difficult challenge, but a necessary principle for receiving God-given courage. To offer prayers of thanksgiving in the tough times is to be subservient to His divine plan for us. It's a vote of confidence in His ability to indeed cause "evil" to boomerang upon our Enemy.

Psalm 50:13-15 shows how deeply God longs for thanks. "No, I don't need your sacrifices of flesh and blood. What I want from you is your true thanks; I want your promises fulfilled. *I want you to trust me in your times of trouble, so I can rescue you, and you can give me glory."*

That's a fairly direct statement, don't you think? Instead of living in an "if only" world which denotes regret, unhappiness and dissatisfaction we are to offer thanks. An "if only" mindset and heartset can nurture anger and rebellion to the point of disobedience. Often we become obsessed with the "if only" ... as we're cleaning house, driving, taking care of the children or doing a multitude of everyday tasks.

Soon our focus is solely on the "if onlys" and not on our faithful Heavenly Father. Anything that causes us to shift our spiritual, mental and emotional allegiance from Him onto other things is detrimental. He says clearly in the preceding verses that true thanks produces true trust in Him.

Jean has declared over and over that when she feels overwhelmed by her circumstances, she thanks God for His watchfulness and faithfulness as a husband to her and a father to her children. She has been an effective vehicle of the Lord's love to her children and now to grandchildren.

Living in Complete Faith

There is a woman recorded in Genesis chapters six through nine whose name is not mentioned but whose life could have been filled with many "if onlys." Her obedience, however, became an essential avenue through which her entire family was saved. We only know her as Noah's wife. What a woman of trust she must have been.

To say that Noah, his wife and children lived during wicked, difficult days is an understatement. Unearthly creatures were wandering the earth, marrying human women and producing offspring who were evil, vile monsters. God was disgusted at the sinfulness of man and gave the people 100 plus years to mend their ways. Humankind had broken His heart but because He is a God of grace, He gave man time to repent—a relatively long time.

Instead of people repenting and improving their behavior, Genesis 6:11 says God observed the world to be "rotten to the core." His solution was to wipe every living thing off the earth and begin again. Noah and his wife must have been parents with great depth of character and divine convictions as they and their children were the only ones righteous on the entire earth at that time.

The Lord provided plans for their escape from His judgment upon the earth, instructing Noah to build an immense vessel to float above the flood waters that would cover the earth at God's command. The boat was to be 450 feet long, 75 feet wide and 45 feet high. There were to be three decks—bottom, middle and upper—with skylights all around the top, and one door in the side of the ship.

Up to that time, some historical experts believe that it had never rained. Imagine the ridicule Noah was subjected to as people observed his daily mission. Along with putting up with their cruel jokes and their questioning his sanity, he had a rather old body—a 500-year-old one! Mrs. Noah could have said, "Noah, I can't take being made fun of. The neighbors' opinions are very important and they won't invite us to their parties if you continue to act like a crazy man. Besides, Noah, you're too old to be doing that. Why don't you just retire and act your age. This ship is an impossible dream, an absurd one because after all, there's not even any water around here to float the thing. If only you would listen to me!"

That is what she *could* have said. Instead, indications are that she supported her husband as the Lord included her and her children in His rescue plans. Each time the Lord gave instructions to Noah for their salvation, He mentioned her specifically.

If she had chosen to undermine her husband's (and God's) plans, undoubtedly they would have all been lost. Noah would have probably become disobedient and given up their means of rescue. He would have abandoned ship!

It took Noah almost 100 years to construct their life-saving vessel. After a century of hard work they went into the ark. God ordained that a pair of every kind of animal make its way to the lifeboat, along with seven pair of every species of bird and seven pair of certain sacrificial animals.

I mention the number of animals because Mrs. Noah had to put up with all levels of noise, odors and messes everywhere! They all spent the first week closed up in the ark before one drop of rain fell. Do you suppose she nagged poor Noah as to why, why, why were they doing such a senseless thing? "What will the neighbors say now, Noah?"

I don't believe she did because God was careful to include her in His plans even though the Bible does not record His ever talking to her directly. God spoke to her husband and he spoke to her. For her, the process worked satisfactorily.

The ark was their place of residence for over a year, theirs and the animals', don't forget. It must have been a difficult, frightening experience, one that tested her patience and mettle many times. When the waters of the earthwide, totally destructive floods receded, the huge vessel came to rest on the top of a mountain.

Again, Mrs. Noah could have griped and complained about such matters as the selection of their parking place and the neighborhood, but she joined her husband in a Sacrifice of Thanksgiving to the God who spared her and her family. The Lord instructed her sons to have numerous children, to repopulate the earth. Hence, from her three sons came all the nations of the earth. What an overwhelming gift—so many grandchildren she lost count! Her courage was divinely blessed because of her attitude, and her deeply obedient faith in the Lord.

So, too, Jean's tried and tested faith in her Lord has provided her with a constant supply of strength when the flood waters have swirled around her family. Her refuge from life's storms has been knowing that Jesus Christ is always there—to forgive, to love, to be merciful and to keep

His promises. Just as God promised Noah and his family, by the sign of a rainbow, to never again destroy the earth by water, so too He has shown Jean over and over that His purpose is not to destroy but to save.

As you give Him your "if onlys" and offer thanksgiving, He'll show you His reality every day you live. As Psalm 12:6 says, His promises are sure. You might not always see the rainbow, but you can always know He's beside you.

Steps to Becoming a Courageous Woman

1. Write down the most well-used "if onlys" in your life.

2. Read Genesis chapters 6–9, and record the times there would have been opportunity for Mrs. Noah to say "if only."

3. Pray, asking the Lord to replace the "if onlys" with the ability to give thanks *in* all circumstances.

4. Memorize Psalm 12:6.

***Determine not to live
in the fantasyland of "if only."***

***Consciously decide
each day not to allow your
problems to rob you of your
rightful portion of joy.***

*The Lord himself is my inheritance, my prize. He
is my food and drink, my highest joy! He guards
all that is mine. He sees that I am given pleasant
brooks and meadows as my share! What a wonderful inheritance!*

—Psalm 16:5,6

11

Joylessness: Result of Misplaced Trust

Both of the women discussed in the previous chapter knew they could trust the God to whom they belonged. They had the faith to believe they were heirs to His goodness and mercy.

When we become members of God's family through receiving Jesus Christ, the abundance of blessings we receive from Him is beyond comprehension. And the exciting fact is that we do not need to be departed from this earthly life to inherit our full measure. All of His attributes can now flow through our lives if we choose to recognize them.

His love, peace, patience, servant-like spirit, compassion, peace, and Presence are qualities that could not be purchased for all the money in the world. Yet Christ already paid the price in full by His sacrifice on the cross. In doing so, He willed us His life.

If you had a rich relative who went to his or her attorney and had a will drawn up naming you the beneficiary of

1 million dollars, that person would have to die before you could claim your inheritance. The money would be yours only if it was specified in the will and witnessed. It is obvious that the will is a very important document because it contains the deceased person's instructions on how to dispense with his or her estate.

My husband Rich has had clients pass away who failed to finalize their wills or continued to delay having one drawn up. The confusion and havoc created by this omission has caused many family feuds, and they are not anything like the TV game show with the same name. These family fights are responsible for broken relationships and hard feelings that sometimes go on for years.

Aren't you thankful God did not leave us without a will? We have His Word, the Bible. In it He specifies what belongs to us if we are members of His family. One of the greatest portions of our inheritance is the joy that becomes ours. We have to decide, however, whether or not to receive it. Jesus Christ longs to give you His joy, but you have to desire His gift.

Have your problems robbed you of joy?

I believe God has a huge sack of joy for me every day. An amazing process takes place when I choose to receive it and be a channel of His joy to others—the sack always remains full. On the days I fail or hesitate to receive it or do so half-heartedly, the bag empties.

Perhaps that's a simplistic analogy, but the more we receive and give away the more we have of His unexplainable joy. There are numerous events each day that try to steal our joy. Often they are very minor, such as a complaint from your husband about his favorite shirt not being ironed. Or maybe your children fuss about the meal you worked so hard to prepare.

Molehills Become Mountains

When I first began to ski, the mountain did indeed seem formidable. Even the "bunny" hill was a killer! My pride took a beating as I was completely at the mercy of those two long skinny boards and gravity, not to mention the cold weather and rope tow. Some "friends" said the chair lift was much easier so I believed them and headed for the lift.

I was somewhat apprehensive as I waited in line, but it really did not look all that difficult. That is, not until I was rudely smacked by the chair as it came around to scoop me up. It left some dandy bruises where I sit. With my skis dangling and my husband hanging on to me, I faced the next dilemma—how to get off at the top?

I encountered that problem sooner than I wanted to as the couple in the chair ahead of us disappeared out of sight and their empty chair came around. I had only an instant to think about my predicament before my husband shouted, "Get off!" I tried to stand as the chair pushed me forward. The incline was steep and icy so naturally I fell backwards on my newly-acquired bruises. Horror of horrors, a post the size of a telephone pole loomed in front of me as I careened down the ramp.

It was as if my body was implanted with a homing device. I zeroed in on that post and found it dead center. Limply, I lay there in embarrassment, praying my husband would call the ski patrol to rescue me.

No such luck! Rich skied over easily and in a sickeningly cheery voice assured me I was doing fine for my first time. I wasn't bleeding so he did not call the ski patrol. That left only one way down. I had to stand up again, with help, and inflict more punishment on myself.

My friend Carolyn demonstrated for me in an easy, fluid manner how one keeps the skis together and guides them where one wants them to go. It sure did look easy, so I took off. But it was *not* easy and effortless, and I soon discovered it was impossible for me to turn. It was not a post I hit this time, it was a large fir tree, for which Oregon is famous.

I remember lying underneath the tree with my skis above my head, dangling from the lower branches. I began to cry as I laboriously untangled myself.

I decided then and there to walk down even though all my "helpers" said it was impossible. They were right, so back on went the skis. I fell six more times getting down the mountain and each time I fell, I had to wait for someone to take pity and stand me up again. My pride took such a beating, not to mention my body.

When I finally met the bottom of the mountain, I was greatly relieved to be among the living. I unfastened the skis and tromped through the snow to our little motor home. Once safely inside, I cried from relief, fatigue and genuine gratefulness for being in a secure place. Within an hour I devoured most of the food that we had brought with us.

By the second hour, boredom hit and a twinge of jealousy swept over me as I looked up the mountain and saw many skiers acting as though they were having the time of their lives. I began to talk to myself and became angry at the mountain for defeating me. At my age, then, I knew it was then or never to learn to ski. It was then or never to conquer the mountain.

Before I fully realized what I was doing, I found myself waiting in line for the chair lift. This time I timed the chair properly and managed to get on under control. As I rode to the top alone, I began to question my sanity and suddenly felt physically ill. I started praying aloud for the Lord to help a poor, pitiful human being (me) and to at least spare my life one more time. I'm so thankful He does not turn a deaf ear to desperate people, even when they're taking self-imposed risks on a remote mountain ski run.

I fell six more times getting down the mountain but avoided the pole and the trees. I later began taking lessons and "fell in love" with downhill skiing. As my schedule allows I now go, whenever possible, all winter long.

How parallel to life are the challenges of skiing. Discouragement and fear will enter every difficult situation if we let them. My joy took a beating when I began skiing. I know that it is possible to always have joy and we're told that nothing can destroy it, but circumstances can cause us to feel as though it's gone.

I was filled with fear as a beginning skier, but courage welled up within me when I became determined that I was going to learn. In order for negative occurrences not to rob you of your joy and courage, you must make a conscious decision that, with the Lord's help, they will not.

Perhaps you are not yet facing a huge mountain. But, how well I know, it's often the molehills that defeat us. Whenever I go back to the place I learned to ski, I'm amazed at how easy the runs are that I once thought so impossible.

Practice and determination make the difference. They are two of the key ingredients that go into living each day joyously and courageously.

Not Trusting in Tangibles

One day as Jesus was preparing to leave on a trip, a man came running up and knelt before Him. He asked the Lord what he had to do to get to Heaven and the Lord began reciting the Ten Commandments. At that, the man interrupted and assured Him he had never broken a single law. Christ knew he was sincere and had been trying hard by his own efforts to inherit eternal life. The Scripture says that Jesus loved him but knew what the man was truly depending on for security, happiness and self-worth.

He put him to the test and told the man he would have to sell everything he owned and give the money to poor people. The next step, to follow Christ, probably would not have been too difficult if he could have been obedient to the first one.

We are told that the rich man's countenance fell because he did not have the courage to sell everything and rely on Jesus to be his Source. He left in sadness because he wanted to live in Heaven when he died, but here on earth his trust was in earthly possessions. He could not part with his base of support.

No, the Lord doesn't expect us to sell or give away everything we own, but He does require that tangibles not be our source of joy or trust. It takes God-given courage in today's world not to rely on the material things of life for our well-being, physically or spiritually.

Instead of having a mind and heart attitude like the rich young ruler, how much better to emulate the mind and heart of David when he writes further in Psalm 16:8,9, "I am always thinking of the Lord; and because He is so near, I never need to stumble or to fall. Heart, body and soul are filled with joy."

He knew the secret to having his entire being filled with joy. With his mind fixed on the Lord, everything else became secondary.

Steps to Becoming a Courageous Woman

1. List all the circumstances in your life that are trying to rob you of your joy.

2. Ask the Lord for His courage to meet each situation in a victorious way.

3. Study Mark 10:17-27 and instead of judging this man, use the illustration as a mirror to see if you are trusting tangibles or Christ to be your source of joy.

4. Memorize Psalm 16:5,6. Fill your mind with His Will.

*Consciously decide each day
not to allow your problems
to rob you of your rightful portion
of joy.*

Resolve not to let your faith become weakened by others.

Don't be afraid, for I have ransomed you; I have called you by name; you are mine. When you go through deep waters and great trouble, I will be with you.

—Isaiah 43:1,2a

12

Perplexities, Persecution Prison, and Praise

One of the major problems we discover when we depend on "tangibles" to provide us with courage is that people or possessions are not 100 percent dependable. That's why God in His written Word warns us over and over to trust in Him completely, and not in things of this earth.

*Has your faith's foundation
become eroded by people?*

One of the most important insights David gained in his life is stated again and again in the Psalms in verses such as Psalm 28:7, "He is my strength, my shield from every danger. I trusted in him and he helped me." Psalm 31:1 declares, "Lord, I trust in you alone." Psalm 32:10 states, "Many sorrows come to the wicked, but abiding love surrounds those who trust in the Lord."

Was David saying that only the wicked experience difficulties in their lives, that only the "bad" have negative situations crop up in their days? Of course not! He knew from experience that was not true, yet David declares the Lord is His shield from every danger. Why did he make these statements? In Psalm 32:7 he tells the Lord, "You are my hiding place from every storm of life; you even keep me from getting into trouble!" That's a fairly broad statement and again, we know from reading about David's life that he suffered innocently many times. Yes, there were occasions when he invited trouble, but he was very aware of those times.

Power of Praise

He knew from experiencing the presence of the Lord that he was *secure* in His love, no matter the circumstances. His trust and hope were in God, not the people around him. Praise, therefore, emanated constantly from his lips reiterating his trust in God's faithfulness. In Psalm 34:1 he states his basic philosophy of life when he says, "I will praise the Lord no matter what happens." This undoubtedly was one of the reasons the Lord gave him victory so often. On many occasions he would be badly outnumbered by his enemies but would be anointed with God's courage.

The two principles, praise and appropriating the Lord's courage, go hand in hand. Admittedly, praise often does not come easily when we're in the throes of difficulty, but it is essential to succeeding in our Christian walk.

Do you ever have days when you're tempted to crawl in a hole and pull it in after you? I certainly do! One day in particular stands out in my mind.

The children were on edge and it was all I could do to keep from "coming unglued" as first one was naughty and then the other. Seems like every one of them spilled something at breakfast—juice, cereal, milk, you name it! The topper came when Kendall accidentally knocked the sugar bowl off a shelf in the pantry and its contents were thrown over and onto everything in sight. Broken glass and sugar, quite a combination!

I finally delivered the children to school (thank the Lord!) and was looking forward to the Christian Women's Club luncheon. I picked up a woman who needed a ride and she complained the entire way there, during the meeting and afterwards all the way to her house.

I was really feeling down by the time I walked through the front door of my home, and the first sound I heard was the sound of running water. That puzzled me somewhat, especially since it was coming from the downstairs study which has no plumbing.

I rushed to see the source of the sound and sure enough, water was cascading out of the ceiling light fixture. Strange sight! After rushing upstairs, I made the awful discovery that the toilet in the master bathroom, which is directly above the study, had cracked in two and was freely dispensing its contents.

I ran to the garage to find buckets and the mop and accidentally knocked a jar off a shelf, shattering it on the concrete floor. By this time, my nerves were totally frayed and I was in tears. Why me, Lord?

Some of the ideas from a little book I had recently read on praise came into my mind. One of them involved praising the Lord continually regardless of the circumstances, to lift the feeling of gloom. Our Enemy hates hearing praise to such an extent that he would rather flee and leave us alone.

I started thinking, "Okay, Lord, you know how grouchy I am because of all the 'terrible' things I've been through today, but I'm going to try praising you anyway." I felt hypocritical at first but the more I praised Him aloud, the more honest I became in my praise. Truthfully, it worked and I was able to courageously, victoriously face the remainder of the day.

Paul E. Billheimer has written the following concerning the importance of praise:

> Here is one of the greatest values of praise, it decentralizes self. The worship and praise of God

demands a shift of center from self to God. One cannot praise without relinquishing occupation with self. When praise becomes a way of life, the infinitely lovely God becomes the center of worship rather than the bankrupt self. Thus the personality becomes properly integrated and destructive stresses and strains disappear. This results in mental wholeness. Praise produces forgetfulness of self—and forgetfulness of self is health.[5]

Praise Amid Persecution

A few years ago Rich and I were privileged to assist, to a very small extent, the Underground Church in China. We traveled to Mainland China carrying Bibles and Sunday school materials. You may not totally agree with what we did, but China was just beginning to open up to Westerners. Most of the Bibles had been destroyed during the Cultural Revolution and even though the government claimed to be printing 100,000 copies per year, that was a small percentage of what the demand was and is.

In order to receive one of the government-approved Bibles, a person has to fill out a questionnaire. They are asked to reveal pieces of information such as, "How long have you been a Christian? Who in your family is a Christian? Who on your block is a Christian?" and so on. Then each government-issued Bible is registered so if there is ever another purge such as the Cultural Revolution that occurred during the late 1960s and first part of the 1970s, the Bible and its owner would be easy to find.

The vast majority of Christians in China belong to the unsanctioned house churches rather than the government controlled Three Self Patriotic Movement, which was designed "to free the Christian Church of imperialistic control."[6] Every activity and sermon is closely scrutinized by the communist government.

The Christians in China who survived the holocaust of the Revolution are among the most courageous heroes of the faith the world has ever known. The unspeakable horrors they were subjected to and the strict confines of the law they must adhere to even today could easily be cause for discouragement or even questioning the faithfulness of God, but their commitment to Him remains solid.

Carl Lawrence in his outstanding work, *The Church in China*, describes another prevailing attitude. He recalls many instances of Chinese believers praising God in the middle of their suffering. On one occasion, he writes, a Chinese Christian told him of witnessing the following:

> There was this cart full of prisoners being driven to prison. The people on the street could not see the people inside, but they thought they were awful criminals to be dragged away like animals. The authorities did not want us to see them. "Are they really that sinful?" we asked. Then we found out the truth. These were Christians on their way to jail. They were all handcuffed together and they were happy. There was no dissatisfaction or resentment on their faces. We could hear them singing as they went by, "Lord you are worthy to receive praise. Praise the Lord."[7]

We experienced a very small portion of their humiliation when customs authorities caught us with the Bibles and Sunday School materials. As we stood watching the guards rifle through our suitcases and throw the unwanted contents to the ground, I couldn't help but understand their persecution somewhat better.

Basic freedoms we take for granted are denied not only in China but in many other parts of our world as well. Even with the recent suppression of freedom and democracy in China, people are still following Christ and His teachings.

Dave Hunt in his book, *Peace, Prosperity, and the Coming Holocaust* (Harvest House), estimates there are possibly more born-again Believers in China than in America.

The ability to praise in order to produce courage should not depend on or emanate from the people who are a part of our lives. The Chinese Christians know they cannot base their relationship to the Lord on how others treat them. Many have been betrayed by co-workers, neighbors and even other family members.

When the apostle Paul was called Saul, he was on the side of the oppressor, tracking down and participating in the murder of followers of Christ. I firmly believe the reactions of the Christians he persecuted played a major role in his own behavior later on when he became one of the oppressed. His faith was not weakened by those around him, but was made stronger.

Even though he suffered rejection, beatings and imprisonment, Paul courageously continued to spread the Gospel. In his letter to the Christians in Philippi he writes, "And I want you to know this, dear brothers: Everything that has happened to me here has been a great boost in getting out the Good News concerning Christ. For everyone around here, including all the soldiers over at the barracks, knows that I am in chains simply because I am a Christian. And because of my imprisonment many of the Christians here seem to have lost their fear of chains! Somehow my patience has encouraged them and they have become more and more bold in telling others about Christ" (Philippians 1:12-14).

Importance of Praise

Did you notice the passage referring to courage? The imprisoned Christians lost their fear of the chains and even the people who put them there thanks to Paul. Physically his situation was determined, to the human understanding, by those individuals around him. Yet he knew God was working everything together for his good.

He expressed that confidence numerous times in the Letters he wrote. The praise that came forth from his lips was genuine and a powerful example to all those around him, the Believers and the unbelievers alike. By praising the Lord in the midst of dire circumstances, he was filled with a greater measure of faith, not by the behavior of those around him, but by God Himself.

Paul knew that the courage produced by praise would have several ramifications. To begin with he told his followers that if those who were being oppressed complained and argued, their light would not shine out to a dark and sin-filled world. Then he told them he knew everything would work out for the glory of the Lord, not his own. He also knew he couldn't allow bitterness and anger to take over even though he was being treated unjustly. He admonished them to be servants in their circumstances.

The courage his praise evoked is vividly illustrated in his refusal to stop boldly sharing the Good News of Jesus Christ. Intimidation and persecution only enhanced his capacity for praise and only by him going through his horrendous ordeals would we be the beneficiaries today of his glorious Letters.

One of the many encouraging passages he wrote is Philippians 2:17, "And if my lifeblood is, so to speak, to be poured out over your faith which I am offering up to God as a sacrifice—that is, if I am to die for you—even then I will be glad, and will share my joy with each of you." These words should challenge and remind us that God is no respecter of persons. If He gave Paul the ability to praise and show God-given courage up until the moment of his death, then He'll do the same for us.

Steps to Becoming a Courageous Woman

1. Read Paul's Epistle to the Philippians.
2. Make a list of all the positive statements he makes concerning his imprisonment.

3. Ask the Holy Spirit to point out the areas of your life in which you have allowed other people to cause your faith to weaken.

4. Pray for renewed faith as your life becomes filled with praise.

5. Memorize Isaiah 43:2a and recite its promises during difficulties.

Resolve not to let your faith become weakened by others.

Receive the Lord's forgiveness for any past failure on your part.

I know how to live on almost nothing or with everything. I have learned the secret of contentment in every situation, whether it be a full stomach or hunger, plenty or want; for I can do everything God asks me to with the help of Christ who gives me the strength and power.
—Philippians 4:12,13

13

When You Can't Forgive Yourself

Perhaps it's too difficult for you to identify with the Christians in China and a man named Paul who lived almost 2,000 years ago. "Their courage is admirable, but they must certainly be stronger in the Lord than I. God sure knew better than to place me in China or in the early church because I would not have been able to withstand the pressure," you might be saying to yourself.

When we rely on our human sources of courage, it is easy to become discouraged and downhearted. Failure becomes a part of often quoted litany.

Have you forgiven yourself for past failures?

We become experts in self-flagellation as we beat ourselves with self-doubt. We use the whips of inadequacy, disappointment and fear to defeat ourselves. Our past failures undermine our obtaining or even asking for God's courage. We feel too unworthy. In particular, we Christians expect much of ourselves and then feel we have failed when we don't live up to our own expectations. Our self-esteem takes a nosedive. Our love of self—the healthy preservation variety—disappears. An unhealthy, self-depreciating attitude begins to overwhelm us.

Negative Love: a Dichotomy

Many women who find themselves in abusive marital relationships see themselves through a negative-love perspective. They are unable to love themselves, so they think it's impossible for others to love them.

Through the ministry of *Virtue* magazine's Prison Conferences, I have been able to meet and become acquainted with many incarcerated women. A large percentage of the women behind bars appear to have been involved in unbalanced relationships with men and as a result, were easily manipulated into doing whatever these men wanted in order to gain their "love." In most cases these women were abused as children—physically, mentally, sexually and emotionally—resulting in wounded and damaged personalities. Courage to say "no" to drugs, abuse, prostitution and crime disappeared as they believed the lie that they had no worth.

Tammy was a special inmate—intelligent, attractive and dependent on drugs. She confessed to me one day that because of her habit, as soon as she was released she would always purposely break probation to be returned to the "safe" environment of the prison. She had invited the Lord into her life but because she lacked the courage to put the past behind, receive forgiveness and allow Jesus Christ to open the right doors, she has been on the prison's "revolving door" program.

She penned the following words which poignantly express the ache and despair of one unable to forget past failure and allow the Lord to replace it with His forgiveness and love.

> I tend to dwell on the past,
> and dream of the future,

But who's to say what will end,
And what will last?
I live on to die,
    with my many dreams
And thoughts—I remember,
only to cry
    Holding thoughts in my mind,
With no hope, and no escape
And nothing to find.

What does the future hold,
    Will my dreams come true
        Or just grow old?

Tammy is back in prison, but I pray she will someday be able to indeed put the past behind her and allow the Lord to overflow her with His worth and righteousness. Only when that happens will she be able to say "no" to the destructive, evil plan Satan has been working in her life. Only with God-given courage are any of us able to appropriate His forgiveness for sins of commission or omission, enabling us to forgive ourselves.

On-going Warfare

One of the most difficult battles I face when preparing to speak or write is to overcome the whispers of condemnation for a sin I committed or something good I should have done, but didn't. "Who do you think you are giving advice to others when such-and-such is wrong in your life? Who are you to be addressing a group when your kids aren't perfect! Remember that sarcastic remark you made to Rich? You're writing about courage when you were a complete coward yesterday?"

The whispers go on and on, but that's when I turn to my ever-faithful, well-worn Bible, the most reliable psychology book I have ever read. It says in Romans 8:33,34, "Who dares accuse us whom God has chosen for his own? Will God? No! He is the one who has forgiven us and given us right standing with himself. Who then will condemn us? Will Christ? *No!"*

I know when I hear the suggestions of condemnation they are not from God or Christ, the Son. That leaves the opposing side. I then have to decide whether to listen to or reject the message. I have to believe the Holy Spirit when He assures me that even when I fail, God's forgiveness is faithful and never-ending. Self-forgiveness is often the most difficult aspect of dealing with the past, but the ramifications of not doing so are usually ugly. Dwelling on past mistakes, whether self-induced or forced on us by others, leads only downward.

Failure brings fear, and fear breeds bondage to insecurities. Insecurity leads to unwise reactions which produce negative circumstances and lead to further failure. Do you see the vicious treadmill we climb onto when we don't appropriate forgiveness for ourselves?

Untrue Love

One day over lunch my good friend Carolyn confessed to me that she did not love her husband of several years. As a young girl she had envisioned falling in love with Mr. Wonderful, having a son and daughter, and living happily ever after. Reality had produced a happy-never-after kind of marriage.

I tried to suppress my surprise and dismay, as I had thought they had a nearly perfect life together. Inwardly, I prayed for wisdom as she confessed past failures that eventually led to her willful choice to marry someone she did not love. She admitted her decision was based on her own desire without any concern for God's will. After all, she and Wayne had much in common—tennis, water skiing, golf, movies and the outdoors. She was impressed with his sense of humor and ambition to succeed in life. There was a missing ingredient, however, a genuine love for him.

She fully expected the romantic heart palpitations to come after marriage. When they didn't, she felt she had made a terrible mistake. She began to desire children, believing that was what the marriage lacked. If only there were two children, preferably one of each gender, her dream family would be perfect. So first a daughter and then a son, born 17 months apart, were added to the family.

Wayne's business grew and soon the dream family resided in a dream house. Church, which had been ignored, needed to be included now as part of the facade. That's where Carolyn and I met, so my shock at hearing her confession that day at lunch was understandable.

After drying her tears and expressing her relief at being able to finally share her guilt and frustration with another person, I remember telling her I knew the Lord could forgive her past. More importantly, she needed to know that if she didn't receive forgiveness, she was in a hopeless situation. If she, however, confessed her willful choices, her stubbornness for wanting her own way, and allowed Jesus to intervene in a divine way, there was hope for their marriage. If she chose not to forgive herself, she would not be able to receive God's love that comes as a part of the forgiveness package. It would be by appropriating His love that she would ever be able to love Wayne.

I would like to be able to say that she acted immediately on that advice. However, her experience involved years of turmoil, pain, tortuous events and eventually her desiring her husband's death. When that was not forthcoming, she began to contemplate ending her own life.

Remember that to almost everyone else, they still appeared to be the perfect couple. She would always laugh at his jokes. He seemed proud of the beautiful wife at his side—and they were faithful members of the church.

As Wayne drove out of the driveway one day to leave on a business trip, Carolyn retreated to the bedroom. Something inside her seemed to say, "This is it, Kid. Time to end all the grief." She thought this meant she was to kill herself that night.

The years of keeping up the mask had taken their toll. The years of feeling like a prostitute every time they had relations, hating him all the more, had come to an end. Enough was enough!

She fell to her knees beside the bed and began to cry as never before. The fountain of years of suppression of failure burst open. As the tears flowed, as the prayers and pleading with God went forth, an amazing process began to take place.

Carolyn shared that, "As I asked for forgiveness for all my rotten sins, I began to pray in a way I had never thought to pray before. I asked God to forgive me for being the woman I had been and to forgive me for being the wife I had been for almost 13 years. I finally realized the change could not begin with Wayne, but had to begin with me. I asked God to remove all of the self-imposed guilt from my life. That night I slept peacefully for the first time in years, without medication and without nightmares."

Little by little, she became aware of a change in her feelings for Wayne. She began to love and appreciate him, unconditionally. Other outside circumstances continued an onslaught against their family but Carolyn and Wayne, with the Lord's help, allowed God to continue to strengthen their marriage. They eventually became an inspiration to thousands of others through their sharing on such television broadcasts as the "700 Club." If Carolyn had not given the Lord the freedom to forgive and put past failures behind, she would have missed out on some of His choicest benefits—a good marriage, godly children, and above all, life.

Peter's Parallel to Failure

When Peter failed by denying Christ shortly before His crucifixion, he found himself at the lowest point in his life. His intentions were righteous, to never fail the Lord, let alone deny he even knew Him. Yet one day he had to face the fact that he had indeed failed. How could he have failed after observing Christ perform miracles by doing the impossible in people's lives? How could he have failed so miserably after being the only human to walk on water? Had he really failed after taking part in the feeding of the thousands as Christ divinely multiplied the bread and fish?

While experiencing despair and shame, Peter stood at the crossroads of either asking for and receiving forgiveness or wallowing in self-pity and regret. He, too, wept bitter tears that served to pave the way for healing, restoration and further ministry. The Lord gently let Peter know he had been forgiven and was still in the Beloved.

This is further evidenced by the obvious blessing of Christ upon Peter's life. The Lord's Presence flowed through Peter to others in healing and salvation. On one occasion he prayed for a woman named Dorcas to be raised from the dead, and she was. How could he have prayed and asked for such a huge miracle unless he had full confidence that he had been restored to the Lord.

In moments of condemnation and self-doubt, he would be reminded of the gentle, loving Jesus. He would remember the many occasions when he observed Jesus forgiving unconditionally, even with His final breath. Peter recalled Jesus appearing first to Mary Magdalene after His resurrection. She, out of whom He had cast seven devils, who was possibly a prostitute but who had been the recipient of His forgiveness. He heard Jesus say, "Wherefore I say unto thee, Her sins, which are many, are forgiven; for she loved much: but to whom little is forgiven, *the same* loveth little" (Luke 7:47, KJV). Perhaps Jesus appeared to her first because she loved Him much and needed reassurance of forgiveness.

Peter received that same reassurance. And without that he would not have been able to impart the advice he gave to the Jewish Christians in his first Epistle:

> So be truly glad! There is wonderful joy ahead,
> even though the going is rough for a while down

here. These trials are only to test your faith, to see whether or not it is strong and pure. It is being tested as fire tests gold and purifies it— and your faith is far more precious to God than mere gold; so if your faith remains strong after being tried in the test tube of fiery trials, it will bring you much praise and glory and honor on the day of his return (1 Peter 1:6,7).

When gold goes through fire to burn out the impurities it feels no pain nor has a choice. It is merely an inanimate object. But when your faith is tested by having to face past failures, you will experience rough going for awhile. Just know that like Carolyn, Peter and Mary Magdalene you, too, will reap eternal dividends if you accept the Lord's love and grace. This is a vital step towards courage, both for today and tomorrow.

Steps to Becoming a Courageous Woman

1. Read Romans 8.

2. List the areas of your life in which you feel guilt or condemnation.

3. Ask the Lord to give you reassurance that you have been completely forgiven for past failure.

4. Memorize Philippians 4:12,13 and ask the Holy Spirit to remind you of the truth in those verses whenever you need it.

Receive the Lord's forgiveness
for any past failure on your part.

***Root out any
bitterness or resentment
you may harbor toward
the Lord or other people.***

Do you want more and more of God's kindness and peace? Then learn to know him better and better. For as you know him better, he will give you, through his great power, everything you need for living a truly good life: he even shares his own glory and his own goodness with us!

—2 Peter 1:2,3

14

Courage to Be Holy

Peter came to the place in his life when he recognized the inadequacy of his personal righteousness compared with Christ's. His own shortcomings were graphically portrayed for all to see, especially himself. It was after recognizing his own inadequacies, yet at the same time his worth in God's kingdom, that his spiritual walk took on a new stability.

His vivid example is encouraging for all of us to follow.

Are you harboring bitterness and resentment toward the Lord or others?

We often have no control over our life's events caused by others. But like the well-worn adage says, although we cannot control another person's behavior, we can control how we react. Courage is often needed for coping with or solving difficult relationships, but presumption is too often used. That is, we rush full steam ahead with what we believe will rebuff or punish the perpetrator. Instead of getting better acquainted with Christ and taking on His Spirit and love, we presume we know what's right and act or react in our own power and emotion. The results are often disastrous, making matters worse and producing more unhappiness, chaos, bitterness and resentment.

Excess Baggage from Childhood

Such reactions stem from many sources, including anger and hurt built up over many years. One of the saddest yet most common forms of resentment I see is the parental resentment stored in childhood memories. It's astounding how many adults remember and dwell on deserved or undeserved punishment, family jealousies or seeming favoritism of another, and are stuck at those points of disappointment in their life. These hurts have a stranglehold that keeps men and women hostage even into adulthood.

Individuals bound by such resentments have not been able to grow up or mature because of the experiences brought with them from childhood. Some lug around a huge amount of excess baggage, mentally and emotionally, leaving little room for the Lord.

None of us had a perfect childhood because we were born into a sin-filled world, but we may choose to retain our bitterness or choose to forgive those who have offended us. That may sound simplistic, and yet I believe in a simple faith. Certain biblical truths, such as forgiveness, often become too complicated in their application.

One of the most dangerous ramifications of carrying around past hurts is justification for negative behavior. I hear comments such as, "I know it's wrong but I deserve happiness," or "I know my godly mother wouldn't approve but that's her problem," or "I want to sew some wild oats because I was raised so straight-laced."

In our modern society where absolutes are becoming obsolete, Christians often stretch their spiritual extremities in order to flex their freedom. Due to lack of courage, however, the freedom is abused. Afraid of being called "square," "straight," or "religious," we often compromise Christ's righteousness.

Being a recipient of Jesus Christ's love and life is not based on being good, but once we have willingly taken His life into our own we must show His characteristics to our world. That includes righteous living. The apostle Peter admonishes us:

> Obey God because you are his children; don't slip back into your old ways—doing evil because you knew no better. But be holy now in everything you do, just as the Lord is holy, who invited you to be his child. He himself has said, "You must be holy, for I am holy" (1 Peter 1:14-16).

The "Exception" Rule

One of the principles that is violated over and over where righteous living is concerned has to do with the "exception" rule. It occurs when consciously or subconsciously we act as though God will make an exception in our case. We may say, "He continues to bless me and hasn't zapped me with lightning so I guess it must be okay for me to continue to lie." "Hey, God wants me to be happy and fulfilled so now that I've found a man other than my husband who understands me, what's wrong with that?" "Churches cannot be trusted," some say. "I don't care for the Pastor," others say as they justify their failure to give the Lord His share of their income.

The list of justified excuses for unholy actions could go on and on, but the basic premise for most of them is birthed in resentment and bitterness which lead to rebellion. When those two ugly culprits are around, courage to remain righteous evaporates.

Presuming upon Grace

The apostle Paul knew human nature so well that he warned against continuing in unrighteous living in order to prove God's grace at work after we become Christians. The power to make correct, godly choices becomes ours when we take on the life (and death) of Jesus Christ (Romans 6:1-3, my paraphrase). We do not have to be cowards when it comes to not compromising God's principles. He gives us His Holy Spirit's power to combat temptation.

Dietrich Bonhoeffer, a German theologian who died at the hands of the Gestapo while imprisoned during World War II, could have compromised his faith to save his life. Instead, he lived out the type of Christianity he had written about earlier. In his inspiring work, *The Cost of Discipleship,* he wrote:

> If grace is the data of my Christian life, it means that I set out to live the Christian life in the world with all my sins justified beforehand. I can go and sin as much as I like, and rely on this grace to forgive me, for after all the world is justified in principle by grace. I can therefore cling to my secular existence and remain as I was before, but with the added assurance that the grace of God will cover me.
>
> It is under the influence of this kind of "grace" that the world has been made "Christian" but at the cost of secularizing the Christian religion as never before....
>
> The upshot of it all is that my only duty as a Christian is to leave the world for an hour or so on Sunday morning and go to church to be assured that my sins are all forgiven. I need no longer try to follow Christ, for cheap grace, the bitterest foe of discipleship, which true discipleship must loathe and detest, has freed me from that.
>
> Grace as the data for our calculations means grace at the cheapest price, but grace as the answer to the sum means costly grace.[8]

Bonhoeffer, true to his theology, learned the penalty for not succumbing to cheap grace or compromising his stand for Christ. When his Gestapo prison in Berlin was destroyed in an air raid, he was taken to the notorious Buchenwald. From there he was moved around to other prisons until he was finally executed April 9, 1945, just before Germany was liberated by the Allies. His brother and brother-in-law were also executed by the Gestapo.

He could have become bitter and resentful towards both God and man and cried, "Why me?" Instead he left a rich legacy of writings that reflect his obedience and strength to the end of his life. They show a warm humanness yet an incredibly courageous spirit. He learned the true meaning of Romans 8:35-39:

> Who then can ever keep Christ's love from us? When we have trouble or calamity, when we are hunted down or destroyed, is it because he doesn't love us anymore? And if we are hungry, or penniless, or in danger, or threatened with death, has God deserted us?
>
> No, for the Scriptures tell us that for his sake we must be ready to face death at every moment of the day—we are like sheep awaiting slaughter; but despite all this, overwhelming victory is ours through Christ who loved us enough to die for us. For I am convinced that nothing can ever separate us from his love. Death can't, and life can't. The angels won't, and all the powers of hell itself cannot keep God's love away. Our fears for today, our worries about tomorrow, or where we are— high above the sky, or in the deepest ocean— nothing will ever be able to separate us from the love of God demonstrated by our Lord Jesus Christ when he died for us.

No Blame or Shame, but Gain

One of the outstanding Old Testament examples of courageously choosing to uphold righteousness and not become resentful and bitter toward God is the story of Esther. Here was a young woman who suddenly found herself part of the selection process to audition for a queenship. If she pleased the king, she would be made queen. If not, she would be forever part of his harem, whether she ever saw him again or not.

Apparently, she was very beautiful and intelligent because she stood out among all the women in the realm of 127 Provinces ruled over by King Ahasuerus. She was the Miss Media-Persia of her day, and the king did indeed select her to be his queen. She knew and respected the power of the king. She had heard about the punishment he had meted out to her predecessor, Queen Vashti, when she refused his request to appear at a banquet.

Consequently, the following year when her people the Jews were ordered put to death and their property confiscated by whoever killed them, she found herself in a moral dilemma. When she auditioned to become the Queen her Uncle Mordecai, who was a palace servant, warned her not to tell anyone that she was a Jewess so no one—particularly the king—was aware.

When Mordecai requested that Esther use her influence to talk the king out of his decree of death to the Jews, she knew that according to palace protocol her life could be at stake if she even went into the king's presence unannounced. That alone could cause her doom, but to reveal her secret also?

Her love for her people and her trust in God was her impetus for obedience. Instead of growing resentful toward the Lord and others and questioning "Why me?" she believed her uncle when he assured her that God had brought her to the palace "for such a time as this."

She wisely decided not to take action on her own but requested that others pray and fast for three days, during which time she would do the same. Her resolve to do God's will was so great that she was ready to die if need be. She said, "If I perish, I perish."

So it was with fear and trembling but with strength from the Lord she went in to the king and was accepted, so much so that several times he offered to give her half his kingdom. She could have kept her secret to herself and become a very wealthy woman, but instead she courageously made herself vulnerable by setting up a banquet for the king and the Jews' sworn enemy, a man named Haman. He had deviously persuaded the king to agree to the death of the Jewish people.

Because of Esther's obedience and her stand for doing right, her people were spared certain death. This involved thousands of lives, as the Jews were scattered all through the Media-Persia territory which stretched from India to Ethiopia.

At the banquet the king learned the ramifications of what Haman had talked him into—that the death order would include Esther. Consequently, because of her courageous effort, Haman's wicked plan boomeranged on him and his family. Esther's and the Jews' enemy was himself put to death.

Time after time, if we would stop compromising with our Enemy and make holy decisions, even if it means becoming vulnerable, our world, our church, our family and our own lives would be enriched. Peter was correct when he expressed the formula in the opening verses of this chapter. When we know God better, He's the one who will enable us, through His power, to make the correct decisions to live a truly righteous, holy life.

Steps to Becoming a Courageous Woman

1. Read the Book of Esther.

2. Make a list of Esther's courageous acts.

3. Pray, asking the Holy Spirit to point out areas that you may be justifying wrong actions. Confess any resentment or rebellion.

4. Memorize 2 Peter 1:2,3 and ask the Lord for wisdom in how to apply its formula.

> ***Root out any bitterness***
> ***or resentment you may harbor***
> ***toward the Lord***
> ***or other people.***

**Refuse to retreat
from life or use
human avenues of escape.**

*For God has said, "I will never, never fail you nor
forsake you."*

—Hebrews 13:5

15

The Keys to the Penitentiaries of Life

___

In the imprisonment of their lives, both Dietrich Bonhoeffer and Esther found the key to unlock the door to freedom. Not physical freedom necessarily, yet freedom from succumbing to hopelessness, despair, resentment and failure. My pastor has said that God views this entire world as a giant penitentiary. He alone has the keys to unlock the bondage enslaving mankind.

Through His "Key," Jesus Christ, we do not have to compromise the godly principles He long ago set in motion. We no longer have to wallow in self-indulgent pride, pity or unrighteous behavior. We are free to pursue holy living, which is possible by securing God-given courage. If we do not habitually seek His courage for the way in which He would have us live, our good intentions and resolve will disappear. We then are likely to use other means as an escape from our discouragement and fear. For most of us, it's inevitable.

Do you find yourself retreating from life?

Avenues of Retreat

There are several well-worn avenues of retreat. I'll touch upon a few of the more popular.

Retreat through sleeping a disproportionate number of hours a day is one of the most common forms of withdrawal from an undesirable situation. If we're asleep, hopefully we will not have to face reality. The same goes for over-medicating. In our pill-oriented society, this is an easy hole to crawl into.

A close friend was in the prison of valium addiction for 11 years as a young mother, even though she was a Christian. The damage to her, physically and mentally, was compounded by the negative way it affected her entire family. At the point of impending death, she grabbed onto her last ounce of faith and the Key became her Savior. He unlocked the drug's stranglehold. Slowly but surely the Lord mended, strengthened, healed and delivered her from the imprisonment of her retreat and its disastrous results. She is now a constant source of inspiration to all who know her.

Another form of retreat and withdrawal is shopping to excess or whiling the time in shopping malls. Buying items one can't afford in order to feel better is a trap to be avoided. Spending great chunks of time shopping, even if nothing is purchased, is often an escape. There may be times this "innocent" activity can serve a useful purpose temporarily as a release valve on a tense situation. The harm occurs, however, when it becomes a permanent lifestyle to the exclusion of more beneficial activities.

Avoiding interaction with others, shutting ourselves in prisons of our own making, is literally retreating from life. Again, there are times when it's okay to isolate ourselves for a short period of time. But if it becomes a habit of long duration, we become islands in our own little oceans. What a lonely, depressing, futile existence. It is interesting to read in the apostle Paul's letters that whenever he mentioned his residence as prison, he also mentioned individuals he had been witnessing to concerning the Truth of Jesus. Even in his imprisonment, he never retreated from life.

One of the most well-used forms of escape from negative circumstances is watching television constantly. Again, while some television is worthwhile, if abused it becomes a detrimental device of escape. This escape is far too common in our culture, especially among young people.

By the time an average American child graduates from high school, he will have ingested 18,000 hours of television—7,000 more hours than he spent in the classroom. He will have viewed 22,836 sitcoms; 350,000 commercials; and witnessed 13,000 killings.[9]

TV's greatest damage is inflicted by the mixed messages it feeds us. For example, commercials for cigarettes and liquor are not allowed, yet we see "stars" consume both regularly on television dramas. Also, is it really all right to kill the "bad guy," even if done without benefit of legalities? We often see "justice" reenacted in this fashion.

Children's escape into cartoons is filled with smashing, zapping, socking, bashing and annihilating the character we don't like, with super-human powers. The most frightening results are the now-blurred lines of reality and fantasy, good and evil, God-power and monster-power, truth and falsehood.

Dr. Brandon Centerwall, a member of the psychiatry faculty at the University of Washington School of Medicine, after seven years of study and research of television's effects and influence on viewers, published a report that contained many shocking findings. He said that television "is a factor" in about half of the 20,000 homicides and numerous other violent crimes that occur each year in the United States. He said at a recent news conference that, "While television clearly is not the sole cause of violence in our society, and there are many other contributing factors, hypothetically if television did not exist there would be

10,000 fewer homicides a year." Centerwall said regions of the United States that had widespread television before the rest of the country also saw earlier increases in homicide rates.[10]

Television is sometimes referred to as "The Plug-In Drug," the title of a book written by Marie Winn. For women, our "plug-in drug" may be used to vicariously have an affair, cause us to see our own lives as boring and mundane, and to give us insecurity complexes concerning our beauty and worth.

There are many other avenues and methods for withdrawing from reality. As I said earlier, they may not be harmful if used only on a temporary, limited basis. The danger is in long-time reliance on any one of them.

Perfect peace or perfect panic?

Isaiah 26:3 promises that, "He will keep in perfect peace all those who trust in him, whose thoughts turn often to the Lord!" Did you notice that it says *perfect peace*? What a blessed state in which to reside. There is, however, a condition placed upon it. Notice the word "trust" again. It keeps coming up in our discussions of obtaining God-given courage. When we totally trust the Lord and not ourselves, instead of being filled with worry and distress, we will see how He can enable us to keep our thought-life centered on Him.

In Isaiah 21, Isaiah confesses what happened to him when he was gripped by fear. He writes, "My stomach constricts and burns with pain; sharp pangs of horror are upon me, like the pangs of a woman giving birth to a child. I faint when I hear what God is planning; I am terrified, blinded with dismay. My mind reels; my heart races; I am gripped by awful fear. All rest at night—so pleasant once— is gone; I lie awake, trembling."

Can you identify with any of his symptoms? Stomach ache, feeling faint, despair, erratic heartbeat, sleeplessness, tremors. If that isn't being afraid, I don't know what is!

When I first read those verses I said to myself, "Is that the same fellow who wrote Isaiah 26:3 about trust and the secret to peace of mind?" Sure enough it was, so I went back over the chapters in between and discovered a few facts about Isaiah.

First of all, after hearing God's voice and taking advantage of God-given courage, Isaiah obeyed and delivered God's message at great peril to himself. Secondly, after observing the destructive power of sin and disobedience, he reiterated by contrast the wonderful plans of God for those who are faithful. After contrasting the two opposing sides, he chose the Lord's and learned by experience that by trusting Him he gained peace and strength.

In verses 12 and 13 of chapter 26, Isaiah makes this simple but profound statement, "All we have and are has come from you. O Lord our God, once we worshiped other gods; but now we worship you alone."

When we retreat from life through oversleeping, over-medicating, overshopping, overeating, "over-teeveeing" or over-anything, those escapes become our god. Whatever we spend the most time doing and is all-consuming in our lives becomes our idol. This may not be an intentional, conscious decision but the result is the same. For that reason alone, retreating from life due to lack of courage is not a permanent answer to the difficult times.

Our trust turns to terror, our peace to panic, and our faith to failure when we retreat. To appropriate courage we must go on the offensive against our Enemy. However, we do not go on our own strength, nor do we go unarmed and undefended.

No Armor for the Backside

In Ephesians 6:10,11, Paul reminds us that, "Your strength must come from the Lord's mighty power within you. Put on all of God's armor so that you will be able to stand safe against all strategies and tricks of Satan." Then he tells us to use God's armor in the fight—the shield of faith, the helmet of salvation and the sword which is God's Word (Ephesians 6:10-17).

When the side that is losing the battle retreats, they are usually running away exposing their backside. Since no armor is mentioned that would be worn on the back, we'll assume that Paul did not have retreat in mind. Neither should we!

Whenever I get discouraged and tempted to retreat, I read Psalm 24 (aloud if possible) and once again I am reminded that my King of Glory is invincible in battle. That means he has *never* lost nor will He in your situation or in mine.

There's a simple chorus I love to sing to myself when the arrows are flying and I feel vulnerable to attack. It says, "Jesus never fails, Jesus never fails, Heaven and earth may pass away, but Jesus never fails." How true that is, for as this chapter's opening verse says, "I will never, never fail you nor forsake you." That fact alone should be reason enough for courageously facing our circumstances.

Steps to Becoming a Courageous Woman

1. Make a list of the areas of your life in which you may be retreating.

2. Make another list of the areas of your life that you need the Lord to unlock with His keys.

3. Pray, asking the Lord to restore or renew your faith in His armor to stand and fight and not retreat.

4. Memorize Hebrews 13:5 and trust in His promise.

*Refuse to retreat from life
or use human avenues of escape.*

Life is treating me poorly these days, and
I am sick. Sick of the life I don't understand,
Sick of watching my feet move, and asking why.
I'm tired of running from place to place....
      So tired I want to die.
Will life give me a chance, a chance to live
And breathe the life unseen?
Will I live before death takes hold,
Or die the death of life unknown?
        Written by Tammy from prison

Know that the Lord has already given you a hope-filled future.

Go ahead and prepare for the conflict, but victory comes from God.

—Proverbs 21:31

16

Bleating Sheep and Braying Donkeys

Let's suppose you are in a position of retreat today. You are probably feeling more uncertain than ever before and are asking yourself, "What's wrong with me? I don't want to be here!" Rest assured, you are normal. Wherever you are physically, emotionally, mentally or spiritually, your Creator knows your situation.

This chapter's opening verse implores us to prepare for conflicts, for they will occur, as sure as the sun comes up every day. And this preparation needs to be done ahead of time. Chaos will result if it isn't. Have you ever tried to prepare a meal when everyone was so hungry they began grabbing food and gulping it down before it reached the table? Well, it's a maddening, confusing situation.

To have the courage to face reversals, we must be prepared in advance. The heat of battle is the wrong time for a soldier to be scurrying around looking for his weapon and ammunition. So, too, we need to always be spiritually prepared to meet the Enemy when he comes.

In Chapter 15 we briefly discussed the armor we need each day for the battle. We should adorn ourselves with this protection 24 hours a day, not try to find it in the middle of the conflict. If we are not outfitted for spiritual warfare, there will be times we will become so discouraged we will lose hope for tommorow.

Are you looking toward the future?

If we don't prepare for the negative circumstances that will most assuredly come our way, our hope will diminish or die in the midst of our struggles. Hope, by definition, is a desire accompanied by expectation; one that gives promise for the future. When a person's hope is gone, it's as though they are dead inside. There may be times when the weight of your sorrow becomes so great you do feel lifeless within, and that you do not have a single ounce of courage left. My friend Tami has surely known that feeling.

Down But Not Out

Tami and Greg were high school sweethearts. She called him her "superstar," and at 6'6" tall, he excelled in every sport in which he participated. His dark hair, handsome features and broad smile made Tami proud beyond words to become his wife.

Within their first year of marriage, a beautiful baby boy was born and became their pride and joy. They both loved being parents and were an inseparable unit except for their jobs. One Sunday morning, however, the dream came crashing down. The telephone rang and it was one of Greg's friends wanting to know if he would like to play basketball.

On her way to wake Greg, Tami stepped into baby Tyson's nursery to check on him and sensed a strange, cold feeling. An awareness that something was dreadfully wrong enveloped her as she screamed for Greg to come. When Greg pulled back the blankets and took the baby in his arms, Tami immediately noticed Tyson's limp body and knew he was dead.

When they met with the minister the following day, Tami admitted to being very bitter and unable to even pray. She was in the middle of the most desperate battle of her life, totally unprepared. After the funeral, depression and resentment became uppermost in her life until one Sunday, at the urging of a friend, Tami went to church. There she heard for the first time with her spiritual ears, the message of Jesus Christ's love for her. She could hardly wait until the altar call to accept His love and forgiveness. Greg recommitted his life to God at the same time.

They continued to have their ups and downs as they worked through their deep sorrow. Tami became involved in a weekly Bible study but Greg kept to himself, not allowing anyone to share his grief. He was, however, looking forward to beginning his football career and education at a major university.

One dark misty night, Tami had to work late. When she arrived home to a darkened house the same cold feeling of dread she had experienced with Tyson swept over her. "Oh, God, where's Greg?" she prayed.

She found out around 1 A.M. when there was a knock on the front door and a policeman standing under the porch light gave her the news that Greg had been involved in a fatal accident. "No, no, no," screamed from her lips. All perspective of life and reality was slipping away. She would surely awaken from the nightmare soon.

Reality began to sink in the next day when she realized there was another funeral to arrange. She was only 19 years old. After Greg's service, she did not become bitter but she admitted to being confused and questioned whether the Lord really loved her. Even though she received encouragement from her many friends, she still experienced deep depression and tried to find solace in alcohol and drugs. She thought of suicide many times.

During one of a series of sleepless nights, she knew she had two choices. She could either sink lower in the pit and kill herself or she could move up higher in the Lord and be a better person, not a bitter one.

Tami writes, "In June 1982, I went to church and confessed my feelings and failures to Jesus. I knew He never left me but He seemed to stand aside and let me find out that I needed to depend on Him. He loved me and wanted to lift me to Himself and give me a big hug. So I let Him. It felt great!" In the intervening years, it has been exciting to watch Tami grow in wisdom and stature with God and to observe a life filled with Christ's love and joy as she ministers His caring to everyone she meets.

The battles Tami faced, and they were huge, caused her to become prepared for any future conflicts she would encounter. Her future has become one of hope and assurance that in the small conflicts, as well as the seemingly insurmountable ones, the Lord is there to provide the needed tools for courage.

She had to choose which path her life would take—despair and death or hope and Heaven, where she knows she'll be reunited someday with Tyson and Greg. What a blessing—to have *eternal* hope!

Hope-Filled Promises

Throughout the Scriptures, the Lord has given us promises of hope. In Jeremiah 17:7 He says, "Blessed is the man who trusts in the Lord and has made the Lord his hope and confidence." Ecclesiastes 9:4 states emphatically, "There is hope only for the living." "Therefore my heart is glad, and my glory rejoiceth: my flesh also shall rest in hope," declares David in Psalm 16:9 (KJV). In Psalm 39:7 he writes, "And so, Lord, my only hope is in you."

The New Testament also holds numerous declarations and promises of hope. In Paul's Letters, he writes of hope from first-hand knowledge. In Romans 8:24,25 he more clearly defines hope when he writes, "For we are saved by hope: but hope that is seen is not hope: for what a man seeth, why doth he yet hope for? But if we hope for that we see not, *then* do we with patience wait for *it*" (KJV).

In Romans 12:12, we're challenged to be, "Rejoicing in hope; patient in tribulation; continuing instant in prayer" (KJV). In Colossians 1:27, "... Christ in you, the hope of glory" (KJV) and in Titus 3:7, "that being justified by his grace, we should be made heirs according to the hope of eternal life" (KJV), are two special verses dealing with hope on an eternal level, not possessing it solely for the present.

Peter echoes Paul when he challenges us to, "Sanctify the Lord God in your hearts: and *be* ready always to *give* an answer to every man that asketh you a reason of the hope that is in you ..." (1 Peter 3:15 KJV).

Mary: Genuine Courage

Another young woman whose life was changed forever by God and who learned about maintaining hope through trials was Mary, the mother of Jesus. We first meet her in the Book of Luke where, according to biblical authorities, she is in her early teens. She is engaged to be married and has been faithful to vows of celibacy before marriage. When the Angel Gabriel confronts her with the shocking news that she is going to have a baby, she is understandably frightened and confused but not argumentative.

She could have said to the angel, "What are you telling me? Do you realize how this is going to mess up my plans? This is certainly a most inconvenient time! You must be mistaken! I've heard that giving birth is painful and I'm just not ready for that yet. Please find someone else to have the baby."

Instead she replied, "I am the Lord's servant and I am willing to do whatever He wants." What obedience and trust, not to mention courage to become pregnant by the Holy Spirit while still unmarried. She was willing to face severe social repercussions and pressures.

Her courage resulted from her complete trust and belief in God's promises. She knew of His characteristics, faithfulness being one of the most prominent. If He had asked her to bear His Son, surely it was not a mistake. She had probably spent time, not only in the Temple, but in the quiet moments of her life communing with the Lord God. When the "battle" began she was, unknown even to her, prepared.

We are told that Mary quietly treasured in her heart the things that transpired between her and her Lord. She didn't run around defending herself and her circumstances to everyone she met. She used wisdom and discretion in what she shared with those around her because she knew her circumstances were beyond human understanding.

God was her Shield and Defender as she quietly allowed Him to fulfill His will in and through her. She knew the joy of His one-on-one friendship and caring. Her continual posture of praise produced a positive attitude and a healthy baby boy, the Son of God.

Prior to giving birth, Mary was uprooted by Joseph who, I might add, was also courageous. He stood by her and kept his engagement commitment. He was an honorable man and did not make demands on her sexually. He had to travel some distance to Bethlehem to register for the census and took Mary with him.

She could have protested, (and at this juncture I'm sure I would have) as she was almost full term. But Mary, who was a real "trooper," climbed onto a bony, rough-riding donkey and accompanied her husband-to-be.

Joseph didn't have an opportunity to phone ahead for reservations, so all the hotels and motels were full. One bed and breakfast manager said the only place he had was a barn out back where the travelers kept their animals—bleating sheep, mooing cows, braying donkeys and whinnying horses. No sterile, gowned and masked medical attendants there! The angels must have assisted Joseph, as it was undoubtedly the most thrilling birth ever witnessed by Heaven.

When Jesus was born, Mary and Joseph's difficulties were only beginning. Soon there was a price on Jesus' infant head as the paranoid ruler Herod ordered the death of all new-born boys. This was his solution to a possible threat to his throne, devised after he had talked with three wise men who were trying to find the birthplace of the promised Messiah.

One night an angel appeared to Joseph (not to Mary, which is interesting to me) and directed him to take his little family into hiding in the country of Egypt. Herod became extremely angry when he discovered the wise men had failed to return to report to him the exact birthplace of the newborn King as he ordered. Does this story sound somewhat familiar? Here is another woman who courageously had a child during trying times but obeyed the Lord's directions. (Remember Jochebed?)

Mary could have protested again by crying, "I listened to you before and look where I had to give birth. Joe, I can't possibly travel to that dirty country, Egypt. The people are strange, the weather is hot, housing is the pits, the fashions are out of date, there are no decent shopping centers, the hospitals are filthy, and so forth." I hope you have the picture by now that Mary was a typical woman with a non-typical faith.

She could have offered excuses at every turn. Yet because of her wonderful example of courage under adversity, we have a Savior. She could have allowed her present circumstances to overwhelm her, causing her not to follow God's perfect plan. But then she would have missed the blessing that God bestowed upon her life and still does almost 2,000 years later as we identify in various ways with her struggles and challenges. May we also identify with her courage.

Steps to Becoming a Courageous Woman

1. Examine your challenging situations. Are you placing your hope in the Lord in the midst of them?

2. Are you preparing for future battles by strengthening your relationship with your Savior now?

3. Read about Mary in Luke 1 & 2 and Matthew 1 & 2.

4. List the occasions she showed God-given courage.

5. Pray, asking for the same kind of courage.

6. Memorize Proverbs 21:31 and remember your Source of victory.

Know that the Lord has already given you a hope-filled future.

Accept temporary pruning in order to produce eternal fruit.

Jesus Christ is the same yesterday, today, and forever. So do not be attracted by strange, new ideas.

—Hebrews 13:8,9

17

Temporary Pruning (Ouch!) Vs. Eternal Fruit (Yeah!)

Mary was able to handle the unique challenges of being the mother of Christ, from his Divine conception within her to the culmination of His death on a cross, by being grounded and "centered" in God the Father. "Centered" is a popular term meaning to gather oneself and become steady within. The process of centering is crucial for any individual.

Some time ago I attended a conference on stress management. The speaker emphasized the importance of being "centered" throughout your day. She advised everyone to locate their physical center, stating that for most people it's their belly button. It could also be a few inches above or a few inches below, but it's in that general area. She said that whenever people felt stressed out they should try to pull their thoughts inward and focus on that middle area of the body for several minutes. That would help to reduce stress.

Guess what? This kind of "centering" doesn't work for me, but I've found something that does. Like the apostle Paul wrote in Hebrews, my strength comes as a gift from

God, not from strange, new ideas. Mental games will not reduce my anxiousness nor change my circumstances. What does give me victory in my day is the package deal promised by Jesus Christ through salvation in Him.

I can't possibly earn, deserve, win or merit it through my own efforts. It is a gift, but I must reach out and receive. Paul advises us in Hebrews 13:13 to, "go out to him beyond the city walls [that is, outside the interests of this world...]" to obtain what He has for us. He also gently reminds us in the following verse that "this world is not our home." It is vital for us to constantly remind ourselves of that.

Someone has said that even an entire lifetime is only temporary. We often forget that the Lord uses all the circumstances of our days as a melting pot to shape us into His likeness for eternity. The process is very often uncomfortable.

Are you apt to sacrifice eternal fruit by rebelling against temporary pruning?

Our yard is filled with rhododendron plants for which this part of Oregon is famous. The springtime and early summer bring forth a riot of shades of pinks, reds and whites as the dull green leaves give way to beautiful blooms. All winter the plants are working to develop the trusses of blossoms, but we can't see what they're doing. Oh, maybe we could watch some of this process if we looked through a microscope, but for the most part it's undetectable until it's time for the flowers to come forth.

In our lives, the fruit Christ desires to produce is of number one importance. He has given each of us special gifts; no one has been left out. But we make choices all along life's path as to what we will do with them. Often because we can't foresee anything good coming from our situation, we'll fight the pain that goes with the pruning and shaping.

At home Rich and I have to trim and fertilize our "rhodies" in order for them to remain attractive and productive. If we just allowed them to follow their own course, they would become overgrown, subject to disease, and would gradually die due to lack of nutrients.

We humans are rather like rhodies in that regard. And because the Lord loves us and wants the very best for us, He has to consistently prune and feed us. Our God-given gifts will go to waste if we do not allow the Holy Spirit to produce fruit which will last throughout eternity. Our Enemy will try to do anything and everything in his power to prevent that.

Eternal fruit remains forever and is the primary reason for our existence. If we or the fruit we produce were only temporary, Christ's death would be meaningless. Courage to "ride out" our negative circumstances is vital, keeping the eternal picture, the long-range view in focus. For only then will we see the unique fruit God wants to "grow" in each of our lives.

Misplaced Object of Trust

Rev. Bob Pagett, a pastor friend of ours, invited Rich to accompany him on a trip around the globe to visit various missionaries. They were to be gone five weeks, leaving Bob's wife Charlene and I home to care for our families. At the time, Rich and I had four young children, but I was excited for him to be able to make such a trip.

Would you believe the first Sunday they were gone someone broke into our house and ransacked the master bedroom and downstairs office, apparently looking for valuables? The intruder took what he wanted and departed. Completely unnerved, I called the sheriff's office and within minutes two deputies arrived on the scene. While they were conducting their investigation, I told them I was "husbandless" for the next five weeks and that I felt very vulnerable. They offered a few suggestions to tighten security, but summarized by saying that because we had six outside entrances, someone who was determined could get in no matter what preventative measures I took.

That certainly restored my confidence! Before I knew the full impact of what I was saying, I declared that my Heavenly Father would have to watch out for my family. One of the deputies made the comment that he sure would pray if he were me, then he left. Like I said, they were great confidence builders.

The neighbors promised to keep an eye out for any problems and my sister Linda offered to spend the night. I took her up on her offer. When she arrived a short while later, I looked out through the windows in my front door to see her carrying the biggest shotgun I had ever laid eyes on. She had come to take care of us all right, with her arsenal! The Lord needed all the help she could give Him.

Because we have never had guns in the house, I didn't sleep all night wondering what she would do with the gun if someone did come back that night. I sent her home the next day but she left the gun behind—just in case.

We placed it under my bed and again I spent a sleepless night envisioning the scene if confronted by a burglar. During the night, because I was awake anyway, I had a lot of time to evaluate the promises of my Heavenly Father. Didn't He say He would hide me beneath His wings? Did He not promise to shelter me in the palm of His hand? Was I going to let Him?

Like a child, I cried to the Lord that night and asked Him to enable me to completely allow Him to be my Father. It was uncomfortable, it was disconcerting, it was humbling, but a pruning took place. Our children also learned a valuable lesson in Trust (note the capital T) and the courage He gives us when we're His children.

The remainder of the five weeks Rich was gone I slept peacefully every night and so did the children—without the gun. I firmly believe the temporary pruning and teaching has produced eternal fruit.

A Courageous, Wise, Practical Lady

Abigail was the wife of a wealthy sheep rancher named Nabal. She was beautiful and intelligent while her husband was "uncouth, churlish, stubborn, and ill-mannered" (1 Samuel 25:3). David and his men were hiding from King Saul near the ranch of Nabal. Instead of stealing from Nabal and abusing his servants, David had protected and defended them. Nabal was unaware of this, however, so when David requested a gift from Nabal to be given in friendship, not taken in battle, his request was denied. David then became very angry and he and 400 of his followers strapped on their swords to take revenge on the ungrateful Nabal.

In the meantime, Abigail heard of this situation that was about to bring calamity to her household. The bearer of bad tidings was an employee of her husband. He must have highly respected her intelligence and discernment because he bypassed her stubborn husband and went directly to her. She had the option to flee, leaving Nabal and the servants vulnerable or she could act in courage and reap eternal rewards. She decided to take courageous action—but would not find out until later the full ramifications of her choice.

She hurriedly put together a gift package of bread, wine, sheep, grain, raisins and fig cakes. She packed the items onto donkeys and started toward David's camp. Nabal would surely have disapproved so she did not tell him, risking instead his wrath when he found out later. This was a gutsy lady!

As she rode towards David's camp, she suddenly saw him coming down the road with his entourage. Imagine her terror at meeting this powerful man. He could just say the word and her life would be taken by one of his men, or he could choose to do the task himself. When she jumped off her donkey, she immediately bowed low in the dirt, signifying her humble attitude. This was a wise lady!

Abigail apologized profusely for her husband's decision and asked David's forgiveness. She also assured him that she knew he was fighting the Lord's battles and that he was safe inside God's purse. Don't you love her analogy? This was one smart lady!

David accepted her gifts and her apology and told her to go home in safety. When she arrived home she found her husband had thrown a big party as if he didn't have a care in the world. The Bible says that he became "roaring drunk" so she couldn't tell him what she had done until the next day when he had sobered up. After she finally told him, he had a stroke and died 10 days later.

When David heard the news, he praised God for taking care of the situation through Abigail. Without her actions, he would have had Nabal's blood on his hands. He hurriedly sent for this brave, wise, intelligent woman and she became his wife.

Instead of becoming paralyzed with fright or running away from the situation, Abigail courageously took evasive action. In her speech to David, it is obvious she knew the Lord and His attributes. The courage she showed was not based on human strength. She had to make choices along the way and with the Lord's help, they were the correct ones.

When she said to David during their initial encounter, "The Lord will surely reward you with eternal royalty for your descendants" (1 Samuel 25:28), little did she know that she would be a part of David's household and that the royalty would include Jesus Christ, the promised Messiah. She was thinking of earthly results, but God rewarded her with eternal fruit.

Steps to Becoming a Courageous Woman

1. Examine the areas of your life that you feel are undergoing a pruning.
2. Write a letter to God defining your feelings concerning any pain or frustration involved.

3. Offer the letter to Him as a prayer and release the contents to His love and care.

4. Read 1 Samuel 25 and compare Abigail's actions to any you feel the Lord would have you take.

5. Pray for the same characteristics that Abigail displayed—wisdom and courage.

6. Memorize Hebrews 13:8,9 and heed its warning.

***Accept temporary pruning
in order to produce
eternal fruit.***

I am the true Vine, and my Father is the Gardener. He lops off every branch that doesn't produce. And he prunes those branches that bear fruit for even larger crops. He has already tended you by pruning you back for greater strength and usefulness by means of the commands I gave you. Take care to live in me, and let me live in you. For a branch can't produce fruit when severed from the vine. Nor can you be fruitful apart from me.

Yes, I am the Vine; you are the branches. Whoever lives in me and I in him shall produce a large crop of fruit. For apart from me you can't do a thing.

—John 15:1-5

God-given courage
is a never-ending quest.

Though our bodies are dying, our inner strength is growing every day. These troubles and sufferings of ours are, after all, quite small and won't last very long. Yet this short time of distress will result in God's richest blessings upon us forever and ever! So we do not look at what we can see right now, the troubles all around us, but we look forward to the joys in heaven which we have not seen. The troubles will soon be over, but the joys to come will last forever.

—2 Corinthians 4:16-18

18

Obtaining The Badge of Courage

As I begin this final chapter, I am overlooking the majestic Pacific Ocean beyond a lovely, wide sandy beach. Sea gulls are gliding and darting here and there as they catch the winds in their search for food. In the distance a boat is bobbing up and down as it works its way down the coast in search of better fishing.

I would like to be able to identify with the sea gulls, soaring freely above their circumstances, not bound by the same laws of gravity as I. Why didn't God create us to have arms fashioned like wings to enable us to fly above our circumstances? Well, since He didn't, I can more closely identify with the little fishing boat as it goes up and down and up and down in the water. Because of high winds the past few days, the swells and waves have increased in size. If the water was serene and calm, the boat's journey would be much more easy and smooth.

I have seen the ocean quite calm on occasion but more often than not it is stirred up by the forces of nature. My life is like that. For a while all is smooth sailing, but then without warning the waters grow troubled. Before I know it, I'm plowing through roaring waves.

During the summer of 1987, Rich and I fulfilled a long-dreamed-of and planned-for adventure. To be honest, it was more his dream than mine but when the time came to go I was excited too! We spent part of that summer exploring Southeast Alaska in our 24' boat—just the two of us—and the Lord! As we departed foggy Prince Rupert, British Columbia, we had to commit ourselves and our boat to His watchcare. The navigational charts became like our Bible. If not for their guidance, we wouldn't have lasted one day on the waters without becoming completely disoriented.

The outstanding beauty of Alaska unfolded around each corner—majestic mountains with glaciers often spilling into the water, the abundance of wildlife and fish (some of which we sampled—delicious!) and quaint Indian and fishing villages.

Most of the exploration went smoother than expected, but there were several harrowing occasions, like the time I almost ran over two humpback whales apparently dozing just beneath the surface of the water. The icebergs we encountered while going into a fogbank were also a little frightening.

The most terrifying time of all took place on our way back into Prince Rupert, when the waves became high and irregular as the water slammed into the corner of an island. We could not see from a distance how really dangerous and rough the water had become. Before we realized it, we were being tossed with great force first one way and then another. Our life jackets were tucked away in the cabin and it was impossible to retrieve them because of the pitching and bucking of the boat.

Because Rich has had years of experience operating boats, he knew the rules and procedures to follow in order to get us out of a bad situation. He headed the boat directly into the biggest waves and then quickly turned it around at just the exact moment, allowing the waves to carry us to calm water safely behind an island.

Importance of Following the Rules

Just as we had to adhere to the rules of boating to survive on our trip, so also must God's principles and promises be followed if we are to live lives marked by His courage. For the Christian walk is akin to boating, full of ups and downs and unexpected happenings, yet it can also be exciting, thrilling and full of adventure.

The view of modern Christianity has been distorted by those who make such claims as, "If you're living the right kind of life, bad things won't happen to you," or "You must not be spiritual enough." Come to think of it, Job, in the oldest book of the Bible, was told the same things by his "friends." In Job 5:8 Eliphaz said, "My advice to you is this: Go to God and confess your sins to him." Another friend said, "If you were pure and good, he would hear your prayer, and answer you, and bless you with a happy home" (Job 8:6).

He was told again by a third "comforter," "Before you turn to God and stretch out your hands to him, get rid of your sins and leave all iniquity behind you. Only then, without the spots of sin to defile you, can you walk steadily forward to God without fear. Only then can you forget your misery. It will all be in the past. And your life will be cloudless; any darkness will be as bright as morning!" (Job 11:13-17).

The misconceptions and fallacies of belonging to God began thousands of years ago as we see by Job's conversations with his friends. Of course we do need to confess our sins and turn to God, but that does not mean that after doing so our lives will be cloudless. In fact, our choosing to follow the Lord and His principles may produce more clouds and storms.

After the apostle Paul became a follower of Jesus Christ, he suffered greatly because of his faith. His life's course certainly was not smooth sailing in calm waters. In fact the Book of Acts tells of an actual shipwreck due to a terrible storm that almost took his life. Was the Lord there with Paul or had He turned His back because of Paul's failures?

God did indeed liberally provide the courage Paul needed to endure every humiliation, beating, incarceration and near death experience. The Lord knew that out of the stormy times in Paul's life, his faith and trust would be strengthened as would his resolve to live for Christ.

Paul's Principles to Remember

In Paul's Second Letter to Timothy, he passes on his hard-earned advice when he writes, "Oh, Timothy, my son, be strong with the strength Christ Jesus gives you. For you must teach others those things you and many others have heard me speak about. Teach these great truths to trustworthy men who will, in turn, pass them on to others" (2 Timothy 2:1,2).

In verse 3 he instructed Timothy to, "Take your share of suffering as a good soldier of Jesus Christ, just as I do." He didn't promise him a life free from pain or troublesome times if he would only live a sinless life. On the contrary, he knew there would be suffering and difficult circumstances for this young man he cherished like a son. He knew, however, Timothy would be strengthened by the Lord for whose cause he would endure much.

He wrote in the next verse, "Do not let yourself become tied up in worldly affairs, for then you cannot satisfy the one who has enlisted you in his army." He was telling Timothy not to rely on the solutions and answers the world may have for his particular needs. If he did that, he would take the Lord out of the picture and He would not be satisfied with him. Paul assured Timothy the Lord would never leave him, however. We are assured of the same message—that God patiently waits for us to acknowledge

He's our Captain, particularly if we've acted on worldly advice that has backfired.

Next, Paul advises Timothy to, "Follow the Lord's rules for doing his work, just as an athlete either follows the rules or is disqualified and wins no prize." (Remember Ben Johnson?) The Lord has set laws and principles in motion and it is imperative that we follow them once we become His followers.

If we continually bend or break the rules He has set forth (for our benefit, I might add), there will be consequences. Remember, however, that our Lord has never been defeated and if we allow Him to work, oh, the joy of being reinstated in the race.

In verse 6 of the second chapter of 2 Timothy, Paul says to, "Work hard, like a farmer who gets paid well if he raises a large crop." Note the first two words of those instructions. Work hard! You mean the Christian life is work? It sure is, hard work.

The entire second chapter of the Book of James reiterates the importance of faith going hand in hand with work. James uses Abraham and Rahab as illustrations of the importance of the two attributes for a follower of God to possess. Of Rahab he writes that she was saved because of what she did. Of Abraham, he writes that "he was declared good because of what he *did,* when he was willing to obey God." By faith we are born into the family of God through Christ, but by hard work we show others that we belong there.

Paul concludes his admonition to Timothy by saying, "Don't ever forget the wonderful fact that Jesus Christ was a Man, born into King David's family; and that he was God" (2 Timothy 2:8). Yes, Jesus was a man who struggled while on this earth as we struggle. In fact, it was even harder for Him. But after courageously facing temptation, rejection and execution, He came back to life to ascend once again to Heaven to prepare it for us.

His last words prior to ascending were, "Here on earth you will have many trials and sorrows; but cheer up (or take courage), for I have overcome the world" (John 16:33). We should never forget that He will provide the courage we need for every day we live, if we will just look to Him.

It's Been There All the Time

Remember the cowardly lion in the Wizard of Oz? When Dorothy first saw him he appeared to be in control, bluffing courage by intimidating her, her dog Toto, the Scarecrow and the Tin man. But it was all a ruse. Deep inside he had no courage at all and was frightened of even a tiny mouse.

As the story unfolds, the lion helps Dorothy and her companions defeat the witch, the creatures and the other forces that try to keep them from reaching the Land of Oz. As his courage comes forth, we see he forgets about the danger to himself as he concentrates on the welfare and safety of his newly-found friends. In the end, the lion receives the Badge of Courage because as Dorothy says, courage was there all the time. He just didn't recognize it.

In the same way, we constantly have access to Christ's courage; it's for our using 24 hours a day. God-given courage is ours as we ask for it—realizing His power and minimizing our own. If we are faithful, someday we will receive the precious Badge of Courage from the Captain of our ship. And it will belong to us throughout eternity!

Steps to Becoming a Courageous Woman

1. To crystallize the principles for God-given courage, list as many as you can remember.

2. Ask the Lord to constantly bring these concepts to mind as you meet daily challenges.

3. Read the entire Book of James for hints on living a victorious Christ-like life.

4. Become so familiar with 2 Corinthians 4:16-18 that you'll begin claiming your Badge of Courage.

God-given courage
is a never-ending quest.

Notes

1. Robert J. Wieland, *In Search of the Cross* (Pacific Press Publishing Assoc., 1967), p. 87.
2. Paul E. Billheimer, *Destined for the Throne* (Christian Literature Crusade, 1975), p. 77.
3. Alan Redpath, *The Making of a Man of God* (Fleming H. Revell Co., 1962), p. 118.
4. Billheimer, p. 125.
5. Billheimer, p. 118.
6. Carl Lawrence, *The Church in China* (Bethany House Publishers, 1985), p. 83.
7. Ibid.
8. Dietrich Bonhoeffer, *The Cost of Discipleship*, 1st ed. (NY: Macmillan Pub. Co, Inc., 1949), p. 54.
9. Erma Bombeck, "Kids see good and bad on T.V., but will they know the difference?" *The Seattle Times/Seattle Post Intelligencer,* Sept. 28, 1986.
10. Dr. Brandon Centerwall, *American Journal of Epidemiology,* April, 1989.

Other Good
Harvest House Reading

THE GRACIOUS WOMAN
Developing a Servant's Heart Through Hospitality
by *June Curtis*

This sensitive and highly motivational book was written to
challenge and inspire today's Christian woman to discover
the joy of sharing Christian love and commitment through
gracious hospitality. June shares the secret of being a
gracious woman and shows how to become the gracious
woman God intended.

IN GOD'S WORD
Devotional Studies to Enrich Your Life
with God's Truth
by *Nancie Carmichael*

With a firm belief that the Bible is meant to be a personal
"handbook" for living, Nancie Carmichael began her *personal*
Bible study years ago as a young pastor's wife. Today she is
the copublisher of *Virtue* magazine along with her husband,
Bill, and leads their over 130,000 subscribers in a Bible study
each month. *In God's Word* is the compilation of the years of
diligent effort and care Nancie has brought to the Bible study
column of *Virtue*. Embark on a great *personal* adventure as
you get to know the Lord more intimately through daily time
in His Word.

THE QUIET HEART
by *June Masters Bacher*

In this all-new devotional by June Masters Bacher, each daily
devotional begins with a suggested Scripture reading, and
through anecdotes, poetry, and prayer inspires each reader to
see life with a fresh perspective. A day-by-day "friend" that
encourages a quiet heart so you can come to know God and
learn how much richer knowing Him makes each day.

THE SPIRIT-CONTROLLED WOMAN
by *Beverly LaHaye*

This bestselling book gives the Christian woman practical help in understanding herself and the weaknesses she encounters in her private life and in her relationships with others. Told from a woman's point of view, this book covers every stage of a woman's life.

BE CAREFUL WHAT YOU CALL IMPOSSIBLE
by *John Haggai*

In this entertaining and practical book, John Haggai is out to make "impossible" an obsolete word. For the millions of Americans facing anxiety, an unhappy marriage, a career collapse, loss of a loved one, or any other "impossible" situation, there is a way out, Haggai insists. A self-test for readers is followed by the three secrets of overcoming the impossible which Haggai calls the TOP principles.

ESTHER—A Biblical Novel
by *Ellen Traylor*

A beautiful young Jewess growing up in the courts of Persia's king is swept to prominence as his queen, despite her misgivings. Although unsought and uncomfortable, Esther's stardom was used powerfully of God as she remained obedient in the face of great personal risk to save her people from extermination, thus becoming one of history's greatest heroines. The bestselling author of *Song of Abraham* and *John, Son of Thunder*, Ellen Traylor has masterfully woven an intriguing story of great courage and steadfast faith in Jehovah.

Dear Reader:

We would appreciate hearing from you regarding this Harvest House nonfiction book. It will enable us to continue to give you the best in Christian publishing.

1. What most influenced you to purchase *Courage of a Woman*?
   ☐ Author   ☐ Recommendations
   ☐ Subject matter   ☐ Cover/Title
   ☐ Backcover copy   ☐ _____

2. Where did you purchase this book?
   ☐ Christian bookstore   ☐ Grocery store
   ☐ General bookstore   ☐ Other
   ☐ Department store

3. Your overall rating of this book:
   ☐ Excellent   ☐ Very good   ☐ Good   ☐ Fair   ☐ Poor

4. How likely would you be to purchase other books by this author?
   ☐ Very likely   ☐ Not very likely
   ☐ Somewhat likely   ☐ Not at all

5. What types of books most interest you?
   (check all that apply)
   ☐ Women's Books   ☐ Fiction
   ☐ Marriage Books   ☐ Biographies
   ☐ Current Issues   ☐ Children's Books
   ☐ Self Help/Psychology   ☐ Youth Books
   ☐ Bible Studies   ☐ Other _____

6. Please check the box next to your age group.
   ☐ Under 18   ☐ 25-34   ☐ 45-54
   ☐ 18-24   ☐ 35-44   ☐ 55 and over

Mail to: Editorial Director
Harvest House Publishers
1075 Arrowsmith
Eugene, OR 97402

Name _____

Address _____

City _____ State _____ Zip _____

Thank you for helping us to help you in future publications!